William Bleasdell Cameron

A month in the United States and Canada in the autumn of 1873

William Bleasdell Cameron

A month in the United States and Canada in the autumn of 1873

ISBN/EAN: 9783337208509

Printed in Europe, USA, Canada, Australia, Japan

Cover: Foto ©ninafisch / pixelio.de

More available books at **www.hansebooks.com**

A MONTH

IN THE

United States and Canada

IN THE AUTUMN OF 1873

WILLIAM CAMERON.

ONE VOLUME.

GREENOCK
D. I. POLLOCK AND JAMES M'INNES
EDINBURGH AND GLASGOW
JOHN MENZIES & CO.

GREENOCK:
PRINTED BY ORR, POLLOCK AND COMPANY,
AT THE 'TELEGRAPH' OFFICE.

TO

SIR MICHAEL ROBERT SHAW STEWART, BART.,

OF

GREENOCK AND BLACKHALL,

LORD LIEUTENANT OF THE COUNTY OF RENFREW,

AND MOST WORSHIPFUL

GRAND MASTER MASON OF SCOTLAND,

THIS VOLUME

IS RESPECTFULLY DEDICATED

BY HIS

MOST GRATEFUL AND OBEDIENT SERVANT,

THE AUTHOR.

GREENOCK, October, 1874.

CONTENTS.

CHAPTER I.

The Voyage Forty Years Ago – The Contrast – Bridge of Boats. International Intercourse Resorted to both Natives – A Maritime and Matrimonial Connection – Turtle Dove at Sea – Sunset, its Beauty – A Prize Contentions Sharer – One Sea of Troubles – Death and Burial at Sea – Lifeboat Drill. The Pilot Boat. New York in the Distance – Arrival.

CHAPTER II.

Landing Clean Bill of Health Terra Firma again. "Fancy Fair" – "Black Mail" – "The Bed Bug" – Plenty of Official Aid – Interested in the Race – Brooklyn Ferry. New York Bay and Her over Long Island.

CHAPTER III.

Brooklyn, the Religions of New York. The City of Churches Greenwood Cemetery Its Magnificence Its Gateway and Works of Art – The Burial Plan of James Gorden Bennett of the New York Herald Decoration Day Beecher Chapel and Foundling Hospital.

CHAPTER IV.

New York men Trinity Church, Astor Exchange, the Tweed House – Cool and Moist. Too Northern and Austere. "The Almighty Dollar. Tea "Hearth also Interesting Office Herald Office Mr deceased White Marble House – The Tenement Hall – Fire Brigade. The Central Park

CHAPTER V.

South by Railroad – Railroad matters – The Cars – Republican Dictatorship Advertising Independence Proposing Marriage and Receiving Modern Agencies Medicine Notes on Foreign Land The Coquet

CHAPTER. VI.

Washington City—Hotel Representatives—Hotel Distinction—City Thoroughfares—The Capitol, its Position. Appearance, and Decoration—The Capitol by Night—The Grounds, and Statue of Washington—The Treasury—Patent Office—Bureau of Agriculture—Washington Monument—Smithsonian Institute—Navy Yard—The Extent of the City—Lifting Buildings, ... 51–75

CHAPTER VII.

Baltimore in the Dark—Hotels—Streets—Washington's Monument—Mr Peabody's Gifts—Druids' Park, and its Attractions—A Black Encampment—Dark Prospects, and Voluble Companions—War of Races—Fleeting Reflections, ... 76–88

CHAPTER VIII.

Philadelphia—Old Capital of the Union—When First Planted—Configuration of the City—Relics of the Past—Franklin's Grave—Public Buildings and Institutions—Girard College and Grounds—Seminary of St. Carlo Borromeo—Marble Churches and Palaces—Fairmount Park—The Schuylkill—The Wissahickon Cemeteries, ... 89–102

CHAPTER IX.

Masonic Temple—Its Surroundings and Site—Its Extent and Appearance Outside—Extent of the Craft in Pennsylvania and City of Philadelphia—Interior of Temple—Egyptian, Norman, and Ionic Halls—Oriental Halls—Grand Lodge and Chapter Halls—Corinthian Hall—Knights' Templar Hall—Banquet Hall—Library—Cost of Building, ... 103–120

CHAPTER X.

Philadelphia—Hotel Musical Attendants—Their Formidable Character and Attacks—The Mosquito a Match for Yankees—American Insects—Phases of American Life—Marriage—Divorce—Dress—Early Rising—"Peeping Tom" at the Theatre—Traces of the War—Centenial Celebrations in Philadelphia, . . . 121–134

CHAPTER XI

En Route for Niagara—Bethlehem, Valley of Lehigh, Susquehanna, and Wyoming—Mauch Chunk, the Switzerland of America—Mount Pisgah—The Classic Valley of Wyoming—Arrival at the Falls. 135-146

CHAPTER XII

Niagara—First View of the Falls—Aerial Estimate of their Extent—Best Points for a View—Table Rock at Clifton—Round the Falls—Mrs. Niagara—"Maid of the Mist"—A Daring Run—New and Old Bridges—Goat Island—Whirlpool Rapids—Indian Veneration for the Falls—The Manners of Indian Wives at Niagara—The Falls at Night. 147-172

CHAPTER XIII

En Route for the Capital of Upper Canada—Travelling Economy—Lewiston—Fort Niagara—Lake Ontario—Arrival at Toronto—Great Trunk Railway; its Plant and Cars, Stations and Offices, and Contrivances. 173-185

CHAPTER XIV

Berlin, Upper Canada—En Route—Churches in the Far West—A Moving Homestead—A City in a Wood, and a Wooden City—Its Inhabitants and Commodities—Its Morals and Religious Sects—Passages of rural Life—Magnets and Scotch Idolators—A Run Across the Country to Ayr. 186-189

CHAPTER XV

Guelph, during "the Heather When Planted, and by Whom Appropriated"—Contrast of the Park—Masonic Ceremonial—Troopers and Soldiery—Visit to Waterloo Township—Labour and the Atmosphere. 190-215

CHAPTER XVI

Toronto, its Position — Its Aspects — The City and its Sights—Famous Lions—Its Architecture—Post Office—Osgood Hall—Law Courts—Queen's Institutions—Troops of Arms—The Queen's again—The Hon. Alexander McKenzie, the Scottish Premier—The Lake of a Thousand Islands—The Rapids—Night—Arrival at the City of Montreal. 216-230

CHAPTER XVII.

Montreal from the River—From the Spire of Notre Dame Cathedral—Site of the City—Papal Influence Adverse to Commercial Life—The Teachings from the Interior of Notre Dame—The Pope's Gifts—Picture Book for the Ignorant—Margaret Mary's Pious Dream—Theological Frenzy—Notre Dame from the Square Opposite—The Law Courts—Contrast to Toronto Courts—Public Market—Champ de Mars—Belgravia of Montreal—The Island the Property of the Order of St. Sulpice—Water Supply—The Church of the Jesuits—The Secret Chamber, and its Magical Idol—The Political Power and Piety of Jesuits—Their Reward and Repose in Montreal—Curious Practice—Loyalty in Lower Canada—Civic Frauds by Jesuits—State of Streets in the Evening, ... 230-263

CHAPTER XVIII.

The Rail and Steamer to Lake Champlain—The Prairie—Bald Eagle on the Track—Burlington—Port Kent—Lake George—Arrival at Whitehall, . . . 264-271

CHAPTER XIX.

Whitehall—Old Route and the New—Saratoga and Surroundings—Fashionable Life at the Springs—A Desirable Country—"Checking Baggage"—Arrival at Albany, ... 272-278

CHAPTER XX.

Hudson—Departure of Steamer—Bustle of Starting—Appearance of the Saloon—Extent of Saloon—Passengers' Enjoyment—Gaslight on Board—Refreshment Department—Lower Deck—Provision for Fire and Shipwreck—Appearance of Steamer at Midnight—The River—Fulton's First Steamer—The Hudson and the Clyde—The Bank of the Hudson—The Croton Water Supply—High Bridge—"Sleepy Hollow"—"Sunnyside"—The Palisades—Hoboken—New York—Arrival, ... 279-295

PREFACE.

There are some who think that the Preface to a book is as necessary as the book itself. This may be the case where, as in this instance, there is no great necessity for the book; but when the book exists, one feels there is an imperative demand on the author to introduce himself to his readers in a kind of an apologetic manner, for asking them to take the trouble to peruse what he has been disposed to provide for them. This is all the more necessary, if we are to believe the spirit in which many have written prefaces to their books; for it is but right for one conscious of the many imperfections which permeate his work to ask his patrons to look upon them with as kindly an eye as they possibly can, knowing that to cherish such a disposition is as favourable for the reader as the author.

There have been many books written on the subject of which this one treats, and therefore the inference is easily reached by many that there is little need for more being produced; but I feel that this is urged chiefly by those who have merely heard of the existence of the books referred to, and know nothing of their contents except in a general way. And the fact that many books have been written on this subject of American poultry, it is regarded with much interest by those residing and having connection with that country, and any shopkeeper, artisan, or tradesman has as great a right or claim to submit his impressions and opinions of what he sees as have Sir Charles Dilke, Dr Russell, or any of the reverend gentlemen who write professionally, and who think they are entitled to greater consideration from the masses on account of their positions.

The following chapters have been written mostly from memory, and on that score may contain more blemishes than they otherwise would share were they altogether written from carefully prepared notes. But I have no doubt that the amount of reliable material in them will make them of sufficient interest and profit to any one intending to visit the shores of that great continent, and amply reward those who are at the trouble to peruse them, and if any one fails in this respect, I will regard the fault as my own, and regret that I have not been so successful as I endeavoured to be in my first efforts at providing what I was anxious should prove of some advantage to my readers.

THE AUTHOR.

GREENOCK, *October*, 1874.

THE STATES AND CANADA.

CHAPTER I.

WESTWARD HO!—THE VOYAGE.

WE can remember some forty years ago, when a poet sang "O, why left I my hame?" for the first time, and how many felt the glow of sympathetic sorrow for those who were hardy enough to seek their fortunes in that new world which now offers so many attractions and fascinations to the children of the old. To cross the Atlantic at that time implied the necessity of bidding an eternal farewell to those who were left behind, for the difficulties and character of this voyage were such that the thoughts of return were very remote in the minds of those who had resolved to follow 'fortune's slippery ba' ' on the uncertain shores of a new country. But art and science and indomitable British genius have overcome and have made what was considered at that time an undertaking of some magnitude little more than a pleasure trip; and the best evidence of what I state is in the fact that somewhere about eighty thousand persons have crossed the Atlantic this year on the various missions of peace in the splendid bridge of boats which continually span the restless and seething floods of that great ocean. When so many are impelled from various motives to come from and go across to the new world, we may naturally expect there will be much talk in the different countries as to what has been seen, and we know that very many glowing passages have been written and spoken of the world beyond the flood; and we can easily believe that the Old World has been thoroughly reviewed by the cute, clever and penetrating Yankees who have visited our shores with scarcely any other aim than to spy the land which very many before they visit it are inclined to speak of with that kind of contempt which is the offspring of ignorance, and which is usually dissipated by a visit to the old land from whence they sprung.

I am disposed to think that much good and permanent benefits are likely to be the result of this great interchange of sentiment when it is the result of personally-acquired knowledge; but if certain things are said merely for pictorial effect, the benefits will be but of a doubtful kind.

I have wondered if it were possible to make a description of a passage from the Tail of the Bank to New York harbour of sufficient interest that any one would be disposed to take the time which is needful to peruse it; but to do that it is necessary I should present something of a kind that is of frequent occurrences on board those vessels which carry such great numbers of all classes, and something which I know is of great interest to many who are embarking on a sea of a different kind at the same time.

We sometimes read in the public papers of the marriage of some two on whom the eyes of a large and loving circle were set and who were the admired of all admirers, and sometimes such a notice has concluded with the announcement that the young and loving pair have gone on their marriage tour to the New World to spend their honeymoon there. Such a pair are seen almost every voyage that is taken during the season when such events come off and when such a tour can be enjoyed, and although there are hundreds on board, these turtle doves seem to absorb the attention of every eye and engross the largest half of the conversation which is gotten into during the voyage, and it is not strange that it should be so, for we all know the efforts which are made to be startling and effective when this important ceremony has been newly consummated. It is grand to read in a public journal the notice referred to, but let us follow this new and interesting couple from the time when they come on board and catch the eyes of all who are round the dinner-table for the first time till they cease to be of sufficient interest to the bulk of their fellow travellers. The lady, of course, receives the greatest share of notice. This delicate creature comes on board surrounded by loving friends, and fairly smothered in flowers and leave-takings. She belongs to the family of blondes, and her "get-up" is a miracle of art and exceedingly beautiful. What a travelling dress that is! What a pannier! What a trail! She must have forgotten the enterprise on which she is embarked. And see that head—what a piece of aeriel architecture! and setting at defiance all the laws of that ancient art. Far aloft and on a dizzy pinnacle of blonde hair sits her little hat swaying to and fro like a bird's nest on a tree top, while her little head seems unequal to the task of supporting the wonderful structure raised over it. And then those gems which tremble in those delicate and elastic ears! now they sparkle in the saloon in the evening and shoot their radiance into every corner and create a new light, and before them the lamps only pale their dim and ineffectual fires. Now we are fairly at sea and evening begins to close around, and the wide expanse of water reflects the rich hues of light as the sun sets in a sky all fretted with golden fire;

> And now we see the sun retire
> And burn the threshold of the night;
> And from his ocean lane of fire
> Sink deep beneath his pillar'd light;
>
> We see the purple skirted robe
> Of twilight slowly downward drawn,
> And through the slumber of the globe
> Again we dash into the dawn.
>
> —*Tennyson's Voyage.*

The scene is changed: the land has sunk below the line of vision, and the broad, expanding sea is scanned by the curious eye, which has now no object to rest on beyond the ship and that wide circle of endless water which it now sees for the first time; and one feels as if all the stability of terra firma had gone, and that one is at the mercy of a combination of opposing forces, which are checked and controlled only by the alternations of science and nature. We have left the land behind, and are on the ocean wave where "the winds their revels keep." There are some tourists, who are on the *qui vive* for a storm, and are disappointed if they do not realize their conception of the sublime and beautiful of which a storm is productive; and it is a rare thing that disappointment in this respect is experienced on the North Atlantic, for the wind has freshened into a gale, and the gale to a storm, and we find there are few who want it now that it has come; but want it or not, here it is, and we must feel it, and endure it and must undergo the sublimity of seasickness as part of what is awful and grand in nature. But the observed of all observers, where are they? True, every one has enough to do with himself at such a time, but the strong must support the weak, and as we scramble through the passage to find some seclusion to divest us of what seems so restless as all around we stumble on an open door—open for air, for though the storm rages above, air is sometimes at a premium below, and sea-sickness destroys many of the proprieties. We try to pass, but are obliged to hold on by the door or other fixed woodwork, which are now beginning to mimic our own unsteady gait. And what a change meets the eye! O what a falling off is there! Look at her now, and think of the process! To what favour is she come! Think if you can of the lover, husband, sick himself, trying to hold that beloved head and a basin at the same time, while a pitching, tossing vessel tumbles him over, and spills the contents of that basin on that fair form. He does the best he can in the case, but the vessel lurches suddenly, and the head of his beloved is ducked in the basin, and sometimes he is obliged to hold on by those fair locks he has sworn to love, cherish, and protect. The lofty structure is gone, and the little head, with its scanty covering, remains the sole relic of the previous grandeur. A sad beginning of life this; and we wonder if the announcement in the fashionable journal will compensate for such an ordeal. Is it too much to suppose that many elopements have been terminated by the disgust created by the first two or three days at sea in circumstances like that related?

Life presents a variety of aspects on shipboard even during the short time one is there. The enjoyment of a calm after one has been nearly rocked to

death in the cradle of the deep is worth all the
sufferance of a storm. It is like the return of spring
when winter has exhausted itself in its severity, and
we forget what we have endured as we bask in the
generous warmth and breathe the invigorating air,
and we feel as if our sorrows were over for a time.

> But what thin partitions do divide
> The temple where good and ill reside

Everything is calm and fair and the vessel runs her
steady course, but from below a messenger brings its
tidings that death has been at work and "a baby is
dead." The vessel has braved the storm, but this
little cherub has coursed through the storm of its
brief existence to rest in unclouded sunshine. The
tidings are sudden and startling, but had we watched
and waited by the couch of that young one during
the violence of the storm and rocking of the ship, we
would have been prepared for the sad news. The
mother has never been seen by many of her fellow-
travellers, doubtless for a good reason that tender
flower required all her care and presence. And now
when it is about to be committed to the deep, she is
still unseen. Sunk in her deep sorrow she cares not
to come, she cannot come and mingle with the crowd,
who are anxious to see the little coffin laid into such
a wide grave. It is carried on deck and laid in the
stern sheets of the lifeboat, until the few rough but
needful preparations are made, and after a prayer by

a clergyman, one of the passengers, the little coffin is lowered by cords attached to it till it reaches the water, and then we see it float away a hundred yards or so, and finally settle down to rest in the deep and silent waste of waters of the Atlantic. If the remotest spot on earth had been its resting-place, the mother might on some future day return and see it; but who will be able to find that spot again? We cannot keep a record of it, and it is lost for ever.

While we pursue our uncertain and dangerous course across the Atlantic, there is a satisfaction—such as it is—of seeing that there is a fair supply of lifeboats provided in case of an emergency, but it seems strange to me (and perhaps to others also) that these boats are never used, but kept continually fixed and cemented in their places, which I think is very much against their use or efficiency when wanted at sea. There is a custom or practice in one line, I believe, of exercising the seamen at sea in lifeboat drill, which must be of great service in handling the boats when wanted in a pressing necessity. And this practice should be of the last importance to all Transatlantic steamboat companies, for the bungling which occurs at launching lifeboats is the frequent cause of great loss of life at sea. The wish is, may they never be needed; but needed they are at times, and the more systematically and speedily they can be used when wanted the better. The desire to make speedy passages, and running and keeping up the usual speed in a fog make it imperative that the lifeboat service should receive every attention to make it efficient in the saving of life, and not have the boats mere ornaments for embellishing the deck work of ocean-going steamers.

We are now some two days' sail from Sandy Hook, and we have not seen a sail since the day after the storm, when a vessel passed us with her sails in ribbons. Now a speck is seen on the horizon over the larboard bow, sailing westward like ourselves, and those who consider themselves far-seeing folks affirm that it is the pilot boat, which, after a little, all are satisfied is correct; and a "pool" is arranged as to which of the pilot boats it is, there being some twenty-four in all in this service, and glasses in all directions are trying to make out who is the winner of the "pool." But as the setting sun and the boat are nearly in the same direction, it is some time before it is discovered that the boat is No. 2, the number being about three feet in size, and painted on her mainsail. Shortly the pilot comes on board with newspapers, and we learn what is doing in the world we have been shut out of for ten days, and all are glad to hear that the "Alabama" is safe, but sorry to hear of the circumstance which gave rise to the report of her life buoys being found floating in the Atlantic shortly after leaving home.

On the evening of the twelfth day, far out at sea, we see the reflection of the combined lights of New York, Brooklyn, and New Jersey, on the sky above. By-and-bye the lights at Sandy Hook are visible, and in an hour are passed. The harbour of New York is then gained, and as we are admiring the endless circle of lights all round on the islands of which the bay is formed, the anchor is dropped. A little boat has come alongside, and now commander H. is in conversation with one of the representatives of the press; but as it is midnight we will go to bed, and wait till the morning, when we will learn what the *New York Herald* has to say about the Australia's voyage out to the great emporium of American commerce.

CHAPTER II.

THE LANDING

The stillness and quiet of a night's rest in a vessel lying at anchor compare favourably with that while she is at sea, beating the billow or even vibrating with the motion of five hundred horse-power engines. The refracted rays of the morning's sun were beginning to find their way through the solitary decklight overhead, when I was rudely assailed by the thunder of a donkey-engine which occupied the space just above my sleeping apartment, and as I was at a loss to know what was up—for I knew that the anchor was certainly at the other end of the ship, and this could not be lifting so as to proceed to the landing-stage — I arose, I washed, I dressed, I went upstairs and found that this donkey which was breaking the peace was busy lifting the luggage of the sleeping and dreaming passengers from the afterhold on deck, so as to be ready for a start after we were passed by the doctor. The passengers congregate slowly on deck, and shortly the doctor is seen to leave a wharf on the Jersey side in a small steamer and come on board. There is a clean bill of health and his duties are light, not even so heavy as to require him to relinquish his cigar nor cease smoking. On the other side of the steamer another steamer makes her appearance to carry off the upper ten to the landing-stage, pier, jetty, or shed, or what you will. The baggage is all put on board the small steamer and its owners follow. We are cast off, and in a few minutes we are on *terra firma* again, but prisoners for a little. Here we are called upon to halt and render to all their dues. Tribute to whom tribute is due, custom to whom custom. There are some who would rather be excused, but President Grant grants no excuse in this department of the public service. The passengers are all called up in single file behind one another and told off, while a Custom-house officer goes through rifle practice in every man's trunk. A person who has never seen such a sight or enjoyed the excitement of having his baggage searched for European treasures in an American port, especially New York, ought at once to get a valise, bag, trunk, or portmanteau, and have it stuffed with contraband, and at once start, hear all the stories about it on the voyage, and then undergo it as *we* did. There are all classes undergoing this scrutiny—green-horns and old stagers. And by-and-bye the place is like a fancy fair. Here you see a fine Paisley shawl hanging over the top of a flour barrel, and there a considerable piece of fine silk lying on a like eminence. Here a box of spotless

gloves, and there another fancy article imported for a
friend. One naturally asks why are these things
expressed as they are, and you are told 'you must wait
till the valuator comes.' A business person asks,
"Why is the valuator not here?" But it does not
pay the valuator to be here—his business is not a
rifling business in a trunk, but an open one, the duty
he gets and whereon must find its way to the coffers
of the State. He has no chance of "black mail."
What do you say, sir? Do you mean to say that
these men are not patriots? They ought to be, for
they wear the badges of Fatherland, the immaculate
"stars and stripes," surmounted by the "bald eagle,"
but the eagle is a very greedy creature, and every
man is equal in this country, and hence the country
is sure to prosper. The goods of old staggers are never
hung up as these are. One has ten boxes, three of
which contain nothing, these are laid on the point
of attack, and nothing is found therein. Then he
throws down his keys and says, "Open the others
yourself, as I have some things to look after," but
this is too much for one man to do, and he prefers to
apply the talismanic touch, and the game is secured.
Another is anxious to catch the train for Chicago,
and asks an old stager what he is to do, for his traps
will take a long time to overhaul. 'There is my
card,' said he, 'tell him to call on you at this address
to-morrow,' and the things are passed with an

alacrity that is surprising. "And what am I to do," said another, "for I have some things in my trunk?" "Take that," said his friend, "I have never found it to fail." The purity of the character of Government officials is early impressed on the minds of foreigners. The facilities which exist for the dispatch of business in America are great, if one can only learn speedily enough the method of their application. If your venture is hung on the top of a barrel for one hour in the first instance, you may have it and yourself kept in suspense for two hours on the second, if you do not learn to be more tractable in the hands of your new instructors. Well, perhaps it would be too much to expect the exciseman to be superior to his superiors. Any maladies which are profitable are very infectious in all countries.

The baggage has all been dissected and tied up again, and we are relieved from further Government suspicion. We leave the green-horn in the hands of the valuator, and seek the assistance of a hack to take us to our quarters, or rather to the ferry, for we have to cross from Manhattan Island, on which New York is built, to Brooklyn on Long Island, in one of those queer things called ferry-boats, which are big enough to carry a whole district, houses and all. The steamer comes in bow on, or stern if you will—for each end is either bow or stern—and the passengers rush in like a flood through a gangway about thirty feet

while everything is done here on a larger scale, and
the gentlemen have one side of the boat assigned to
them and the ladies have the other in rooms which
run nearly the whole length of the vessel and the
centre is occupied by horses, carriages, oxen or other
animals which live and move, and anything which
goes on one or two wheels or more. Like the rest of
the crowd, we rush in carriages and all, upon this
gangway, which has an engine in the centre and two
ponderous wheels one at each side and everything is
covered in, and the pilot is on the top of all. It
requires no turning, which is certainly an advantage,
and when it is full, or has waited its time, an invisible
hand strikes an invisible bell or gong, and off we are
carried, carriage and all, to the other side. There are
no such things in this country as public piers or
quays, every company has its own one, and used for
a specified purpose. The ferry-boats pass this one
and there is never an interval of any length of time
that they are unoccupied so great is the traffic of the
various ferries. Two or three boats carry passengers at any of the ferries, and they ply every few
minutes. Out in the bay our attention is attracted
to the number of boats which are engaged in this
particular work, as the islands are numerous around
the bay, necessitating a great number of boats all
constructed pretty much on the same principle, and
forming a decided contrast to the boats on the Clyde,

but the American idea of marine architecture differs considerably from the British idea or standard. Their local requirements have given it a type which looks strange to a British eye. The unseemly walking-beam gives a nice steady stroke and a steady regular motion to the wheel, but it is a feature which spoils the look of a steamer otherwise trim. But it is not possible to impart the appearance of speed or trimness to them, there is so much of them above water, which disqualifies them for going far from home; but I will return to the subject of the American boats again.

At a cursory glance, the harbour offers such a wide field for observation that one does not know where to begin, or whether to begin at all, for you feel a sort of bewilderment, that has the effect of stopping up every other sense—there is such a demand on the eye for the time; for off in the centre of New York Bay you feel you can say without contradiction that you are surrounded by a greater amount of life and commercial activity than is possible for you to be in any other portion of the habitable globe. If we consider there are fifteen or sixteen Transatlantic companies' boats coming in here continually some two or three times a week, it will give one an idea of the extent of that phase of commercial life on the waters and in the city; for, though many of these boats are obliged to lie on New Jersey side, the greatest portion of the business connected with them is done in the City of New York. Then besides these steam, there is a greater fleet of sailing ships from every country in the world doing business with the mercantile representatives of the great Republic: for, though Philadelphia and Baltimore have the connection with the ocean, the facilities which New York enjoys over the others will always keep her what she is—the chief mercantile city of North America. I do not doubt but this fact has a wonderful effect on the Yankee character. It inspires him with a frothy conceit when he has nothing to take credit for. He found these advantages ready-made to his hand and has only to adapt himself to them and secure the profits. But on looking around, it is evident that this city is getting too small for its growing wants and hence we see them putting forth those efforts which entitle them to be considered as trying to do something to enable them to take their place among some of the early nations of the world. On the left two massive piers are growing up, on the shores of the East River, to the height of two hundred feet and shortly an iron bridge will span that river, joining Long Island to New York; ships will be able to sail under it and tramway cars to go over it. so that the compressed growth of the city will yet easily out in that direction and Brooklyn will outstrip the parent city in a few years hence.

There is no end to the number and character of

buildings and public works which are seen from this point. Forts, batteries, towers, arsenals, magazines, navy yards, hulks, ships of war, Russian war vessels getting a friendly overhaul in an ally's dock, hospitals, sugar refineries, graving docks, slips, depots, warehouses, factories, foundries, spires, turrets, domes, are all bristling under a burning sun and a clear sky, which enables you to see a long way with the greatest distinctness. But we are nearly knocked off our bearing, for our boat has run in smack against the landing-place, and we must take the road for it again. We leave our two dark charges to land our baggage and get slowly up Broadway, while we get into a German lager saloon to refresh ourselves, and now we feel in a condition to enter the City of Churches. We get over this dirty causeway, and mount our machine, and in a short time we stop at the private residence of an old friend, a Greenockian, who was my *compagnon de voyage*. We recount our travels, our hairbreadth escapes, and express our gratitude for deliverance; sketch an outline for a campaign on shore, but that can only be prosecuted after the enjoyment of the necessary repose and collation; for we left the steamer in the hope of getting a good substantial breakfast, done up in thorough Yankee style and something worthy of the "New World."

CHAPTER III

BROOKLYN

I CAN'T remember at present whether the order of things is reversed in the West so far as the motives of the people are concerned, in regard to their residences. In our own country the inhabitants go west in almost every case, so much so that a "West-Ender" is always understood to be one of the upper classes. But Brooklyn is not the West End of New York; in fact, New York has no end at all — it is merely circular, or tending that way. Brooklyn is on the east side and is the quarter where the great majority of the aristocracy dwell. It is the chief city on Long Island, and from the confines of one district to the other runs for some six miles or so, containing about a hundred thousand people. There are more than a dozen other places on the island, but they are of minor importance, being removed from the great centre. Next to it being the abode of the wealthy and the retired merchants, it is distinguished for its churches and its preachers. As in all fashionable resorts, where wealth and culture are found, they are very nice as to the kind of persons who shall be their instructors on theological points; and this is very much the case in all the large towns and cities. I must say it is not at all clear to me why Brooklyn has been called the City of Churches. I failed to see or learn that there were more churches than were wanted, or that the people were more inspired with the devotional attributes than elsewhere. I doubt not but that they are all very good citizens, as they ought to be, but some of their public men get into scrapes as well as the members of other connections, and now that we have claimed that human nature is the same here as in any other place in the Union, let us see if there is anything in the neighbourhood that is worth saying a word in favour of—if there is anyone whose fame has reached the other side that will be worth seeing. Well, there is famed Beecher. We will keep that in view for Sunday, and in the meantime let us look at the exterior of the place.

I said I did not see anything that was indicative of an excess of the religious devotional element in the people, for I am not disposed to attribute the building of churches to any higher motive than has been given in relation to the person who "loved his nation and built them a synagogue;" but we can, where there is taste, genius and liberality displayed in those structures, throw in our small contribution of admiration and gratitude to the men who have beautified their cities with so many fine examples of architectural art ; for it is such works which make

foreigners entertain a high opinion of the people of
any country, and is a compensation to the traveller
for his labour in seeking what is noble and exalted,
either in the world of art or of nature. The streets
are narrow and very long, and the distances are great
from the sights one is anxious to overtake; but the
tramway cars obviate this, and you can go over four
or five miles for the small sum of twopence-half-
penny, or a shade less, the sum being five cents, and
considering the small charges the tramway stock is
the best investment in the country to original holders.
This is the result of the great numbers who take
advantage of this means of locomotion. The distances
are great, and the money seems plentiful with all
classes who spend it freely. The cars are much the
same as they are here, but about twelve inches wider
inside, giving more freedom to move in and out.
There is no travelling on the top of the cars. The
excessive heat in summer and extreme cold in winter
may account for that; but one coming from this country feels disposed to get up from the fact that the
top of a car or 'bus is the very best spot for sight-seeing.
But shadow and shade are sought for there, and are
indispensable to all; for the sun would ultimately
lick up and reduce to a crisp those thin wiry creatures
we see carried to and fro by every car which passes,
were they to expose themselves unnecessarily. There
is no other feature that calls for remark in connection

with the cars themselves. The structure of the way is very inferior to what it is in this country. This may be occasioned by the inferiority of the streets themselves, for if there are some things in which we are behind the Yankees, it is not in streets or street-making. I think in that particular they are a period commensurable with their independence behind us. In some matters they urge their juvenility as a reason, but we will not presume to say what the reason is in this case. The severe frosts, the heavy falls of rain, the hot weather, are all against them, for I know they have tried everything but the right thing, and when they discover that, I doubt not but that their roads will be equal to any in creation. A thunderstorm, accompanied by rain, which falls so heavily, that a few minutes suffice to turn the level streets into canals, and the cars seem to be going along the surface of the water. There are some of the cars which are open and have eight seats, to which you enter by the side of the car, and are protected by a flat covering on the top and curtains let down at the side in winter; and they are very airy in hot weather. And again, the number of the cars is something that is quite astonishing. You may go to any spot where they are run, and where the traffic warrants it, of course, and you will find that they pass at the rate of a hundred in an hour. At some places it is greater, for it is not an unusual thing to see four lines of rails

...one street, and by allowing an interval of two
minutes for each car, you have an estimate of the
extent of the traffic. This only applies to the great
centres in Brooklyn.

There is no special feature about the public buildings that calls for any remark. Indeed Brooklyn
makes no assumption to be renowned for anything
remarkable about it but its churches and its unap-
proachable and magnificent Cemetery of Greenwood.
There may be other cemeteries in the world famed
on account of their striking historical and classical
incidents and associations, but for position, design,
natural beauty, and rare examples of memorial and
architectural art, it has no parallel anywhere. It is
some two miles out of the city, and the cars took us
to the gateway at the northern entrance. But one
cannot pass in if he has any relish for the fine arts
without first contemplating the allegorical beauties and
lessons on the stone-work of the gateway. The
structure is of Gothic architecture, over one hundred
and thirty feet in length and one hundred and six
feet high to the top of the middle spire or tower.
There are two small spires or towers, and the latter
naturally form two openings. These openings are
filled in with trusted Gothic arches and quatrefoils,
and in the centre are two shields, on which are figures
of Faith, Love, Hope and Memory. Below, on the
panels of the arches are bas-reliefs of the "Raising of

Lazurus," "Raising of the Widow's Son," "The Saviour's Entombment," and "The Resurrection." In the centre are a clock and bell; the latter tolls on the occasion of a funeral. The centre tower or spire is supported by flying buttresses, which run through the building between the *Gothic arches over the gateway. The wings of the gateway are taken up with cemetery offices, &c. This gateway is only used by visitors on foot or in carriages; funerals go in and leave by an entrance for funerals only. The cemetery extends for miles, the space occupied by it being some five hundred acres. There are lakes, reservoirs and fountains, chapels, catacombs, sarcophagi, and an endless variety of all kinds of monumental works; and these are almost wholly composed of white marble. I will only refer to one as a sample. There are many such, but as the person to whose family this belongs has a world-wide notoriety, I will take it. The person I refer to was a Scotchman, who went to the States over forty years ago, from Aberdeen, and was distinguished for his indomitable fortitude, his chequered social career and tortuous political proclivities, and his ultimate success in his enterprise in connection with the *New York Herald*. James Gordon Bennett bought, and his family possesses, one of these beautiful spots in this cemetery, and the group of fine sculpture work which is enclosed within the palisade and balustrade is worth going a long

way to see. On a pedestal, about six feet high, is an
angel about the same height, holding aloft an infant
while on a cushion beside the mother is kneeling
with her hands clasped and face upturned to heaven,
as if giving away her child. The work is of the first
order, was executed in Italy, and of the finest Carrara
marble. The lace shawl which is thrown over the
mother's head, and the rich full folds of the satin
dress, are wonderful works to come from a mallet and
chisel. And we wonder, also, how they retain their
purity and sharpness, exposed as they are to the
weather, and to the floating germs of vegetation, for
the place is thickly wooded in the vicinity of this
group. It would fill a volume to describe the various
works of interest which are here strewed all over
the immense space, the groves full of romantic
beauty and fragrance, their silence only broken by
the quick and monotonous music from the myriads
of grasshoppers which dwell on the grassy slopes of
the avenues, and the soft cadences from the falling
waters at the fountains, as they are borne along on
generous breezes through the lanes and alcoves of
this City of the Dead. There is one feature connected
with the cemeteries which I will refer to when I
have the subject on hand. It does not apply to
Greenwood, however, so much as it does to other
burial places which lie near to the great battle-fields
of the Union, here however, you are instructed for

here and there you can see the grave of a soldier, and on it a miniature of the "Stars and Stripes" planted over the body of the dead hero, and once a year, on a certain day called "Decoration Day," the friends, comrades, mothers, wives, sisters, or other patriots, come and plant anew the "Star-Spangled Banner" over the graves of those who fell in the strife between the North and South. In one cemetery I saw what appeared a little army of the dead with a tiny flag at everyone's head. If the advantages in this union are commensurate with the sacrifice of human life, those who decorate the graves will have a sad pleasure in the melancholy act.

We will leave the cemetery, and turn our steps to a plain-looking church in one of the lanes of Brooklyn —a place which forms a contrast with the situation of many of the churches in the city. It is a plain, massive, brick building, like our Town Hall, but not so large. We went in, expecting the Rev. Mr Beecher to occupy his own pulpit or rostrum. The pews are sparsely filled, ominous of disappointment to us. His place is taken shortly by a stranger, and then we feel we have plenty of time to look around for anything that is noteworthy. A very large organ occupies the recess behind the platform. It looks larger than the one in the Town Hall, and the choir is in front of it, and the preacher in front of that again. A bouquet of flowers is set on a small table

at the right hand side which also contains what
books are used. A subordinate gives out a hymn,
which is sung with an accompaniment, the same
person reads any notice of meetings for the coming
week—the collection is made—and the preacher steps
forward gives out his text and the sermon begins.
The singing is done standing, and so that has entailed
a little effort the fans are called into action, and
their gentle breezes pervade the whole church, and
make it comfortable. The heat must be awful when
the church is packed, and possibly it is a wise pre-
caution on the part of the minister to absent himself
when the weather is very hot, and may be productive
of longevity in pastor and people. It may be asked
why this divine has such a poor church. Compared
with some in the city it is large, airy, and the
acoustics are good, and I believe he prefers the
money laid out in more useful and charitable ways.
No man in the ministry has the power of raising
money equal to him for monuments of his work are
to be seen as we pass along. We take the cars and
ride two miles or so into the country, and we come
to a large quaint Gothic palace built with variegated
bricks and stone with commodious grounds surrounding it, and every appearance of comfort. We
ask what kind of institution it is, and we are told
it is "The above Foundling Hospital." Such are the
kind of works this man engages in. Their magnitude

shows his great capacity, and he has always some one on hand, and these take him from home at times, to glean in other and wider fields than are in Brooklyn.

CHAPTER IV

NEW YORK

I once heard a person remark that to be dropped in the streets of London without a penny in one's pocket and without a friend would be a calamity of no ordinary kind. I presume it would be much the same were a person to be set down in Broadway in similar circumstances. In the first place, you feel yourself lost in the wilderness of stone, bricks, marble, and iron which surround you; in the interminable and crowded arteries of the city which stretch from you in all directions, and lose themselves in the distant perspective; and to pursue one's way through the busy, bustling, striving and struggling crowd is a task of time, requiring some energy and caution, and you naturally feel disposed to contemplate all this pressure and bustling activity from some quiet spot where you can get the outline of the city and an idea of its extent and character. You look about and see a church of Gothic structure — Trinity Church — with its spire peering over the tops of all the adjacent buildings, and you inquire if it be possible to get up on this Babel to see this goodly land, which stretches around studded with temples, palaces and workshops, and clear sparkling rivers and bays crowded with richly freighted argosies and barges, of divers size and rig. We climb the dizzy height and scan the expansive map, which lies stretched out far below, and mark the land running far out and joining the waters of the Atlantic, and the far off hills and promontories, lying robed in the golden radiance of the noonday sun. The streets chiefly run at right angles with the avenues, which are the chief lines of the city. Broadway is seen from this point to great advantage, and it is here where one gets the correctest notion of the extent of the trade of the city, so far as that can be got by the use of the eye, and the outward evidence of trade and commerce. A short way from here, to the right, are the greatest number of offices connected with the shipping, and across that part of Broadway there are about 200 telegraph wires, connecting the Exchange and banking-houses, and the various mercantile firms of this city together. The Custom House, the Treasury and Post Offices are all near to this part of the city, and Wall Street is the great centre running through the whole. One building strikes us—it is of white marble—and for the site on which it stands one million dollars were paid; the sum, also, which was expended in its construction must have been great. There is an imposing and chaste grandeur about the building which is productive of

feelings which, I suppose, one would be influenced
with were he standing near to a great mystery. It
is a banking-house and called "The Drexel House"
for one of the proprietors. These white marble
palaces are common enough in New York. Within
a short distance of this one are many such, but the
Drexel House is freed from the crowd and so makes
a rare and noble example of marble work. Some of
these white buildings stand out in bold relief when
surrounded with buildings composed of brickwork.
There is one thing which is worthy of remark and
noticeable from an eminence like this. There is no
smoke to be seen over all this great city except from
two or three public works, which must be burning
some other thing than coal, for the coal here has
no smoke and hence all the white buildings retain
their purity for a long time indeed, and this exemp-
tion from smoke and soot influences everything in the
city, and great cleanliness is the result. There are
very many buildings which are of great interest, but
the building which obtains the greatest amount of
interest is the Stock Exchange. The front-streets
of this great community are wrapt round it, for all
speculate in stocks of one kind or another, and here
the life-blood of this great commercial centre flows
out from the Exchange by the thousand wires
which we see spanning the streets and principal
commercial houses, and in all places where merchants

most do congregate are to be seen these small telegraphic intelligencies speaking out the state of the various stocks at all times of the day. One can see them in the windows of offices and on the side tables in restaurants, going click, click, while the white tape runs out as the machine records the price of gold or other stock. They seem to be thorough adepts at figures and often consulted by the passing thousands, and are the great oracles of the destinies of the New Yorkers. A visit to the Exchange has an interest of a kind to one not commercially interested. You are aware of the fact of being introduced to where business is being publicly carried on; but if one were to go in, ignorant of the character of the place, he might take it for a mad-house, especially if business were at fever heat when he chanced to be there. The privilege of being allowed to do business at the Exchange is purchased at a large sum—perhaps there is no favour, for even that is a purchasable commodity—for all things resolve themselves into negociable material through the medium of the centre of power—the "Almighty Dollar." This lever makes and unmakes "States and Constitutions." The law is all powerful or relaxed as it is applied; the judge is severe or considerate in proportion to the prospect he has of a sensible return for these judicial qualities. The sword of justice is put into the scales, and her eyes are only sealed when her

favour is bought. All this kind of business, however,
is not done on the Exchange; you can discover knots of
busy speculators on the public streets selling stock as
in the Exchange, and conducting themselves in the
more sensible and decorous manner of the two. I have
spoken of buildings of stone, brick and marble, but I
forgot at the time to refer to another material which
is well represented in all the chief streets of this and
other large cities of the Union. Marble and iron
are the materials from which the largest and finest
blocks of buildings are composed. I have referred
to a Bank, and will only refer to an Insurance Office
and to the office of the *New York Herald*. Possibly
these structures, and the business conducted in them,
are unparalleled in the world. Through the kindness
of a gentleman, formerly of Greenock, I was introduced to a number of gentlemen in the 'Equitable,'
and was shewn over the establishment, and finished
on the top of the building, which is 114 feet high,
and from this an excellent view of the city is
obtained. The roofs of nearly all the buildings are
flat, and are applied to various purposes. On this
there is an observatory for astronomical and meteoro-
logical studies, and others for various purposes are
in the building, but the main portion of it is devoted
to the business of the 'Equitable.' In the main
flat is a large office, rising to the height of 40 feet or
thereby, and the ceiling is covered with stained glass

and is supported by large pillars of variegated marble.
The desks of the officials are all enclosed by light rails
of ornamental bronze work, and communicating with
one another by gates of a similar description. Round
the main office are offices and retiring rooms, dining
room, and lavatories, and consulting rooms; and
above, about midway, is a balcony, with entrances
to other apartments of the officials; but the extent of
the whole may be best conceived by the amount of
business done by this Society, which amounted last
year to the enormous sum of 51,911,079,00 dollars,
and their transactions in cash being for the year the
sum of 8,420,044,86 dollars, being the largest of any
office in the Union by seventeen million dollars. In
this, like many of the larger modern buildings,
although there is a stair case, the easier method of
ascending and descending by means of an elevator is
adopted. There is one on each side, and all folks
when rising in the world take the advantage of them.
The office of the *New York Herald* is not so high
above the street as the "Equitable," but there are
two storeys below the level of the street where
machinery is kept and heavy work is done. The
third floor or storey is devoted chiefly to receiving
advertisements and similar work, and a portion is
occupied by shops, as is the case with nearly all large
buildings. The revenue from this kind of occupancy
is so remunerative that all proprietors let the street

or part of the street storey as stores. The five or six
storeys above are printing offices, and occupied by the
various branches connected. Next in style and
magnificence to these marble and granite piles are
the iron buildings, and when painted white, as they
usually are, they can be put in close juxtaposition
with the marble for beauty and general design and
appearance, when these are sought and not strength.
The iron ornamental buildings in Brooklyn New
York, Philadelphia, and other large cities, are finer than
the marble ones for sharpness of ornament, freedom
of detail, and general or intestural arrangements, and
for lightness. I omitted to state, when speaking on
the subject of the *Herald* office, the extent of newspaper printing in New York, as may be inferred
from the army of boys who are engaged in the sale
and carriage of them in various ways. One can
scarcely believe it, but two years ago the number was
set down at 9000, and we naturally presume the
number to have increased since that period. This
branch of industry, to which so many of the juveniles
devote themselves, must tend to much good in
providing labour for so many who would run the
risk of being captivated by some of the less reputable
companions to which so many of the boys apply
themselves. We might go along Broadway and the
Bowery, and find much that is interesting on
examining the exterior of many of the buildings in

these thoroughfares. Perhaps if I take one. We have seen a bank, an insurance and a newspaper office. Now, at the other side, we have a large mercantile house belonging to a gentleman who began life as a schoolmaster, and who was asked not long ago to become Secretary of State by President Grant, when he first accepted office. This white marble repository of dry goods is not inferior to the others I have referred to. It is six storeys high, and it occupies a block 100 or 152 feet, being the whole block bounded by four streets. There are entries at all the streets, and you enter by a stair or elevator to whatever flat you wish to do business in. In the centre of the building is a very large dome, and the entire inside or central part of the building is lighted by it, and the floors are supported by tiers of arches, and between are open balustrading, and in moving round these you can see all the business operations going on inside on all the flats. We can see or learn from this example the great capacity which resides with many of the gentlemen in New York for business, that kind of it which is implied in the character of the place I have submitted; but that is not the limit, for in an old paper I got into my hands it contained the remark, "that the people of Great Britain were at a loss to know who would be able to fill Mr Gladstone's place, if such a vacancy should occur. Here," they said, "we could find thousands

to do so.' All aspire to be civil and political
administrators. The aspirations of those who have
the ambition to feel their relation to political and
civil duties of the States can be discerned at an early
stage. If a child is born within the confines of an
palace in a country where Monarchy is the power of
government the aim would be to fit the scion to fill
the important duties which wait for it in its riper
years. In a Republic every babe is an heir to
imperial honour and power; and it is amusing to
notice the halo of importance that is allowed to fill
and encircle these puny, chattering and spoiled apes
from the time they know anything till the time they
entertain supreme contempt for those who have been
chiefly instrumental in inflating them with unskilled
accomplishments. Let us turn aside and look at a
building of a different kind from any we have noticed
yet. It is of stone, and on the pediment is a figure
of an Indian. It is a common-place looking building,
but other than common-place administrators have
emanated from it. It is the forum where the
"Tammany Ring" digested and matured those
measures which were intended to make their city
and State models that the residue of the Union
would regard with wonder and admiration for purity
and disinterestedness, but now that its benches are
silent, the eloquence of those patriots hushed, and
the fire of their patriotism quenched, why does

not the city go into sackcloth and ashes and wail for the great who have fallen, whose weapons of war have perished?

The streets of New York are superior to any you see in the east part of the Union, but even they are not equal to the streets in our best towns and cities. The traffic is so great they soon get worn out, and I don't know that any great effort is made by contractors to make this kind of work substantial and lasting. There seems to be considerable success in connection with their efforts to make their fire brigade efficient for the speedy extinguishing of fires by introducing facilities for effecting that by every means and agencies. At the stations, of which there are some forty in all, the steam-engines stand fully equipped with fire kindling, horses saddled, and firemen all waiting for the alarm bell; when that sounds, the horses leave their stable and walk into the engine, which is kindled at once, and away the whole rush like an avalanche; and the steam, if the distance is great, is up, and the engine is in working trim by the time it arrives at the fire; there are iron ladders fixed behind the houses, or before the houses if it is impossible to have them fixed behind, and the occupants can ascend on to the house-top and get away by the top of the adjoining house, or descend by them to the ground. These ladders enable the firemen to ascend when their own ladders are not available, and give

them openly facilities for operating on the burning
house.

In this, like all large cities, the channels for
ministering sensual delight are numerous; but in the
Big Susan the delights which most delight a Yankee
are his buggy and his bucephalus. Let him get behind anything with four legs that will only run fast
enough, and then he is at home. He does not seem
to care how the onlooker feels, nor how much he is
concerned for his safety. Away he dashes like a
whirlwind, as if his and the nation's destiny de-
pended on the velocity of his fragile and trembling
machine. In the Central Park one can, on any Saturday afternoon especially, encounter a legion of these
airy, wiry, bristling chariots rushing with stampede
impetuosity along the crowded drives of that delight-
ful and extensive park. Here you can find all classes
that are at home, those who have not gone to Saratoga
or Long Branch, but prefer the crowds around the
band stands, or love to lounge in the grottoes or
groves, or over the stone parapets by the lakes, and
watch the swans gliding along the glassy mirrors of
water, and the rich images of the small launches, as
they sail past with their canopies of gay colours and
infantile crews, or admire the golden fish sparkle in
the fountains, as they startle at the falling of the
crystal spray. There is a representative of every
nation to be found here but one especially with fea-

tures as decisive as if you had found him by Babel's streams thinking of his Zion. Crowds of Jews are here, for this is their Sabbath, and their worship is done, and they have come hither to spend the remainder of the day, and admire the beauty of the scene and works of art. On the sides of the avenues are to be seen statues of Shakespeare, Scott, Burns, and Morse and other new world celebrities; and on the stoneworks at the stairs at the archways are allegorical *bas reliefs* of the Seasons, admirably cut on freestone, and surrounded with a great variety of Mosaic entablatures and other ornamental filigree work. The lawns are wide and ample, and the youths are engaged in all kinds of sports, and the youngsters are sporting and bounding like gazelles in every glade; and on the retired spots pic-nic parties are holding their orgies, and gathering new strength, vigour, and life to arm them for their labours of the coming week of toil. A sylvan retreat like this must be a fountain of life to the toiling thousands of a city like New York.

CHAPTER V

THE RAILROAD SOUTH.

THERE are many things about New York worthy of a passing notice, but as my intention is not to write a history, and as similar things will fall to be noticed as I prosecute my journey in other places, I will refrain from noticing them at present. There are railways communicating with New York direct but in going South one has to take the ferry-boat and pass over to New Jersey side and go from there by rail, and in doing so I have arrived at the first railway station I have been at in the country; and I feel disappointed, for I am quite impressed with the fact that this one does not do justice to the great country that it is in. Other institutions have offices which do them justice, and impress the foreigner with their commercial importance; but perchance this one may be exceptional. One naturally thinks that marble and iron might be used in their construction, and as this one is virtually a city station it ought to have something of the relative grandeur of the city about it, and hence you are more disposed to find fault on this account. But it is otherwise with the care when in their pristine freshness. There is evidently an effort made to make the cars both handsome and comfortable, and even luxurious. The interiors of them are finished with much taste, the fittings are magnificent, especially in the palace cars: for in a country where so much liberty, fraternity, and equality prevail, and has greater facilities for carrying out improvements than in this country where so many distinctions are recognised and accepted as legitimate, you can hire the emigrant car, the ordinary, or the palace and sleeping cars. In the palace car you are attended by a coloured gentleman, and you can have anything your taste may dictate. You can fare sumptuously all the day, and at night your palace, by the stroke of the black attendant's wand, is transmogrified into a palace of another kind, where you can commit your weary limbs to rest, and allow yourself to be lullabied to sleep by the deep and sonorous music from the vibrating metals below. The interiors of these cars are draped with hangings, sofas, tables, and everything which is calculated to take the mind of the traveller from the fact of travelling to the comforts of a home. The ordinary car is well fitted, the sofas are comfortable, of which there is one on each side holding two persons, and there is a passsge down the centre affording full and free communication with the whole train, if you are a saloon car passenger. The inside of the car is about 10 feet in the centre of the ceiling, and from 40 to 50 feet long. The whole

upper part of the car is decorated with showy ornament, and the sides are finished in polished woodwork, with inlay or marquetrie. Lamps are hung
from the roof at intervals of 10 feet or so and at
one end you have a stove and at the other you have
a cabinet d'aisance. The exteriors of the cars are done
in the same showy manner as the inside, with beautiful decorations and sometimes the quality and sometimes the destination of the car is painted on it. The
car is supported below by two triple axles, having
three wheels on each, so that if one of them should
break no danger or risk ensues to the train or passengers.

It was night when I embarked in this train of novel
cars, and my first ride and the first ensemble was to me
decidedly novel; there was a general murky gloom
pervading the entire scene, the lamps in the cars only
diffusing a sort of misty glare. Many were running
to and fro looking for the section of the train that
was to be their asylum for the night. Some who
had got into the wrong car were hurrying out to get
into another. Some were busy getting the luggage
checked, and the usual "hurry skurry" was being
enacted from common to quick time, as the train was
about to move off. At last the shrill pipe sounded,
and I left New Jersey for newer scenes in the South.
It is a common matter for a train on leaving any
place to run along one or more streets for a long way

and to provide against accidents all the engines are provided with large bells, which are kept in motion from the time the train starts till it is quite clear of the habitable parts through which it is steaming, and when that is accomplished the train moves off at a steady measure. The speed is much the same as at home, and I never had occasion to note any extra engineering acrobatism by any engines or train by which I travelled.

I presume the Yankees understand the necessity of railroad travellers economising time by the way, on the principle that he who runneth may read, for the backs of railway tickets, and every available spot where advertisements can be seen, are utilised. The plain surfaces of rocks, palings, enclosures, trees, &c., are covered with an array of characters defying the genius of bill-posting to emulate; so that when one comes to any city he does not need to waste his time by inquiries as to where the good, better, and best of everything are to be had, at the cheap, cheaper, and cheapest cost that it is possible to sell them at.

At home when once you adjust yourself in your corner you can consign yourself to your doubtful slumbers in the arms of Morpheus, and feel yourself gently refreshed by a short span of oblivion in the care of that dreamy deity; but only try it outside of the palace, sleeping, or saloon cars, and wake to discover your mistake; for every now and again the

doors at the ends of the cars are slammed and in
stalks a youthful orator who informs you in a sten-
torian pitch that he can supply you with something
for the brain, the digestive organs, or something you
could give away to a friend without entailing an
enormous outlay; and then at short intervals one
considers somewhat plaguy, but as it is productive of
that which enables you to enjoy what is partially
amusing and interesting by the way, you are inclined
to overlook it.

After having parted with friends at the station
and proceeding to still more distant States one
naturally feels disposed to ruminate on the strange
surroundings, strange faces, strange sounds, distance
from home, thoughts of collisions going off the track,
getting telescoped, and finding yourself in the grills
of a cowcatcher or ascending in the moonlight in a
cloud of burning vapour to find yourself shortly
floundering on a shingle roof or paying an abrupt
and unwelcome visit to the dormitory beneath.
Thoughts will make all these fancies intrude into
the domain of probability and of which you find
yourself dragged by a sudden relaxation of speed,
accompanied by a clash, making you feel as you had
waked from a dream. A voice rings into your ears
a name which is familiar to you and you listen for
its repetition; soon the name itself is rung out
without any mistake and you begin to feel that you

have been dreaming, and are on a trip to merry England, when another clash and jerk occur, and the name of Kensington is rung out. You look about, but it is dark, then you try to reflect, but you have scarcely light enough for that, and conclude that you are in the Metropolitan, and you are underground, but by-and-bye you will arrive at Charing Cross, and it is all right. In this half-pleased, half-dreamy state you resign yourself to the future care and guidance of your conductor; contented with this effort to compose yourself, you take another transient dose with the sleepy god, for your rest is now becoming more necessary; but again you start up and find the train at rest, the conductor calling out that the train has arrived at Mantua, and in a confused and bamboozled condition of mind you conclude you are on a foreign tour after all, and shortly you will be sure to meet some of the Gentlemen of Verona as you pass along, since you have been so curiously successful as to get into Italy. And now you begin in a reverie to review and censure the crooked and devious ways of the great people of the great country you are sojourning in; but, after a great deal of cross-examination, you feel disposed to leave them where you found them for the present, until they and you become better acquainted, then you decide the best thing you can do is to take another draught of this curiously mixed

repose while pursuing your tortuous wanderings to the South.

One cannot for the life of him refrain from an effort to ascertain why all this diversity of names of places has taken place, and on the first chance you ask some one whom you consider sufficiently intelligent to enlighten you on this curious, puzzling, and doubtful point, and are told that in all likelihood the first settlers came from places of the same names; but after a little cogitation your perplexity becomes more perplexing, for you reason, who could come from Babylon, Syracuse, or Troy, Nineveh, Carthage, or Athens? From the last certainly it was possible, but not at all likely; but these are fine names and are evidently indicative of a people of taste, learning, culture, of large and expansive ideas, and who are anxious to write a page in the history of the world which will be read by subsequent nations with wonder and admiration, the grandeur and sublimity of whose exploits in the arts of peace and war will naturally dim and eclipse those of the ancient world, and then these places will take the place of the birth-place of the statesmen, the heroes, the philosophers, poets, mechanicians and noblemen who were the chief actors in the drama of life on the stage of the early civilized world.

However, we can sympathize with an aspiring people who are so aspiring for fame and disturb their

which were ranked with the names of these places in olden times, and we ought to hope that all their subsequent efforts and ambition will take their tone and complexion from their high-sounding key-note. Their acts have shown them to be a people equal to the position, circumstances, or situation of the time; and seeing they are so closely allied to ourselves, we ought in charity to wish them well and that they may prosper. We know that many have gone from this country, leaving behind them anything but a blessing. The same may hold regarding other nationalities, and these may have tried to blot out all the instincts, the reminiscences, and associations of their early homes, by adopting names that had no claim but that of being used by one of the early Republics. But, again, there are undoubted evidences of honest representative men, and one feels pleased, especially if he is a Scotchman, on hearing the broad, homely, and distinctively national name of Camlachie sounded out when he comes up to a station, and perhaps after he has been dinned with a succession of names outlandish, unutterable, unmusical, and only serving to bring to memory the days when Red Indians roamed at large through the primeval fields and forests of the great Continent.

Daylight begins to break, and we have run across New Jersey, Pennsylvania, and now we are on the confines of Maryland. We have passed the ancient

capital in the dark, but we will get a chance of seeing
it again after seeing the modern one. Meanwhile,
let us take a look at the country as it throws off the
blanket of night and gradually attires itself with the
color robes of the morning's freshness.

The country is very unlike the people. There are
no great temples clad in verdure, burying their domes
in the fleecy clouds which are floating overhead, but
the land is modest and rising gently, with undulating
hills, crowned and robed with the remnants of wood
and forest which the woodmen, the early settlers,
have spared, and which now serves to beautify the
land. On the broad green patches are the log and
farm houses, and here and there, in some retiring
spot you can see the hut of the squatter, who even
disdains to be the subject of a Republic. He is fain
to use the earth, the sea, the air, the skies, and
patient enough to wait till the proprietor calls for
rent or taxes. There are some fields which give
evidence of labour and culture but rudely and
unevenly finned; others are dotted with roots of
trees which have remained in them for years, and the
ground that intervenes is cultivated and sown with
all kinds of produce. Indian corn always being conspicuous. Here and there the rivers are seen murmuring
and threading their way in the valleys; now and
then you see a bird of gay plumage, but of tuneless
worth, dart from tree to tree. There are no hedges,

and the boundaries of parks, plots, &c., are ill defined. The snake fence is purely a characteristic of the back-wood, and on all railroads thousands of miles of it are to be seen, employed enclosing grounds in all directions, hence the neatness and compactness of our home farms are awanting. But we are now nearing the great centre—the political centre of the great Republic—and the white dome of the capitol is moving along slowly like a snow-clad mountain-top as we near it by a circuitous course. We approach by one of the streets or avenues for a mile or more, and latterly we reach a wooden shed which is dignified by the name of station, but is virtually unfit for a lumber store, and now we have reached the capital by the Pennsylvania Air-line Railroad.

CHAPTER VI

WASHINGTON, THE FEDERAL CITY

WHEN one arrives in this city of magnificent distances he is at once taken charge of by some representative of one or other of its hotels, for there are some half-dozen or so of these in waiting, and when any one appears who is suspected of being in want of a home, these agents of the "bald eagle" are down upon him at once, and unless he shews symptoms of a disposition to be able to mind himself and to paddle his own canoe," it is with difficulty he can shake them off. But sometimes you will allow yourself to be enlisted by their excessive politeness, and then it is clearly their duty "to take you in." I thought if this is the sort of thing it is the lot of all travellers to undergo, I can't be any worse than the rest and with this resolve I got into one of the buses when in a brief space I was landed at the entrance of Willard's Hotel, where I was politely asked to on gross my name and take in the required, then shewn to my apartment, and for the first time I have a chance of seeing the magnitude and greatness of an American hotel. This one is the finest in the city, and is the abode of a number of the Senators and Representatives in the season when Congress sits. But everybody who can get out of the city at this time is out, it being the Congressional recess, and the place has a quiet aspect in every quarter. In this hotel there is accommodation for a very great number of persons, and if ever the house is full it must be a very animated sight, especially at meal times, for the practice or custom, in American hotels, is to dine at the hotel, if not, you are charged as if you did so; but that practice is beginning not to be relished, even by Americans, and hotels are to be found conducted on the European principle of charging only for what you get, and you are thereby not necessitated to attend meals in the hotel you may chance to be staying at. The most distinctive features in the hotels here are the great facilities afforded to both commercial men and tourists. On the ground floor of all the hotels you have telegraph and post offices, newspaper, tobacco and cigar shops, barber's shop, bar room, baggage room, left luggage office, smoking room, lounges, and other necessary conveniences. The baggage, when you leave, has a small brass plate with the name of the place to which you are going attached to it, and you put the counterpart in your pocket; the luggage follows you as by instinct, and when you arrive at your destination your baggage is waiting for you. You don't need to pass a thought

about it, and it is a rare thing thing that there is
any misadventure. I don't know that there is any
other marked difference between the hotels and our
own at home. Their extent, and the fact that many
make them their home, give them a different aspect
and character from what they have with us.

If one were to judge of the importance of Washington from the condition of the public thoroughfares
he would not be very favourably impressed, but the
Executive are beginning to be ashamed of this state
of matters, for pretty generally the streets are undergoing a thorough renovation and proprietors are
groaning under the pressure of taxation imposed to
meet the expense. Occupants do not feel, or rather
do not see it, as proprietors are responsible for all the
taxes, and their collection is much more easily accomplished than with us, for the proprietor is virtually
the tax-gatherer. Washington is somewhat exceptional
regarding its streets and avenues for some of the
American cities, considering the ground to be so
plentiful, have streets that are genuine copies of
some in the old country. But Washington streets
and avenues are very spacious, the avenues radiate
from chief and central buildings like the Capitol for
instance, and the streets run from these sometimes
at right angles and sometimes diagonally. The
avenues are a little after the boulevards of Paris and
they extend for miles in every direction. It is cer-

templated to make this city, at some time, the glory of perfection, the joy of the whole land. But now and again some of the refractory States' Legislatures interpose and question the propriety of doing so, as they consider the capital ought to be near or about the centre of the empire, and advocate its removal to Chicago, St. Louis, or some more western point still; for there is a difficulty in fixing a central situation in such a progressive and extensive country.

There are some of these avenues 160 feet in breadth, and a few of the streets near the Capitol the same. North, South, and East Capitol Streets are the same breadth as the avenues. The avenues are named generally after the States of the Union—the streets by letters and numbers combined, and their regular and open position causes the city to look admirably from any height. The dome of the Capitol is the best suited for this, and it is an object of intense interest, on account of being the meeting place of the Legislative Body of the Union, of marked historical associations, grandeur, and architectural merit. The Capitol stands on a rising ground some 90 feet above the level of the Potomac River, and the height of the dome from the base of the pile is 280 feet, making the elevation 370 feet in all. The original building—the corner stone of which was laid on the 18th September, 1793, by President Washington, aided by the Freemasons of Maryland—is composed of freestone and painted white to tally with the porticoes, which are white marble. The north and south wings were finished in 1800, the date on which the last Congress was held in Philadelphia. But in 1814 the whole of the interior was destroyed by a British military and naval force, and after that date the extension of the entire Capitol was commenced; but the most important extensions took place during the last twenty-two years and the material used during this time was white marble. The entire pile which is 751 feet in length has a very imposing and majestic look with its deep porticoes and endless colonnades of massive pillars, rising tier upon tier, and its allegorical and historical groups of figures at the porticoes and on the pediments and parapets. The original dome of the building was composed of wood, but when the latest extensions were done it was found to be too flat and bulky, and was removed and a dome of iron work substituted, which is a marvel of art, and about 400 tons in weight. On the top of this dome is a figure of "Freedom," composed of bronze and weighs nearly seven tons. In the inside of the dome, and round the circle of its ceiling, is a continuation of allegorical pictures, by the famed Brumidi, in oils, etc. As one would naturally expect, the chief figure in this work of art is the statue of the land surrounded by Liberty, Victory, and Fame trumpeting his glory and telling the

wreath for his brow. Before this group are thirteen female figures, representing the original States of the Union; on the brow of each is a star, and a banner is interwoven, on it being inscribed the motto of the Constitution, "*E Pluribus Unum.*" There are certain floral or cereal symbols, denoting the States they severally represent, and they are geograhically arranged, beginning in north-east with cold, clear tints, and finishing with the warm mellow tints of the south. The central figure of the next group is War, Freedom on one side with uplifted sword striking down tyranny, and kingcraft, and priestcraft —a soldier is trying vainly to hold up the ermine robe; discord, anger, and revenge are in the group. The next group is Agriculture. Ceres is enthroned in the centre with her cornucopia. Young America is on one side, with his cap of liberty *(Le Bonnet rouge de France)*, and he is attaching a pair of sprightly horses to an American reaping machine. Flora and Pomona are in waiting with fruits and flowers. Next comes Tubal Cain or Vulcan, representative deity of mechanics. He stands with his foot on a cannon, and all around are the material forces of death and destruction, the agencies of human devilry, the tools of ambitious tyrants. The next is Commerce, and Mercury presides over the various mercantile interests. In his hand is a bag of gold, and urging, I presume, the immediate resumption

of sea[...] to a great American [...] who is represented. Two sailors are [...], and point to the protecting guidance in the distance. Neptune is the next in this mythological array. As the deity symbolising and presiding over the maritime interests of the empire, he has his trident in his car and his characters, sublimely rising from the deep, accompanied by the beautiful Aphrodite Venus, and cherubs with outspread wings; and the whole band are busy laying the Atlantic cable. Last scene of all, Minerva is seen in the full-fledged glory of her intellectual power as she springs from the brain of the great Jupiter, and an army of attentive and brilliant children of the Union are sitting at her feet and receiving her wise counsels. These are Dr. Franklin the philosopher, Robert Fulton the engineer, and Morse, of telegraphic eminence.

There is nothing of special interest to be noted in the Rotunda until we descend to the bottom of it, and there we see eight large cartoons painted on cloth and let into recesses in the order, and forming large panels, which run round the whole of the Rotunda about twelve feet up or so. On them are represented incidents of interest in the history of the States and connected with them. There is the Discovery of the Mississippi by De Soto in 1541, and the Baptism of Pocahontas, "The Declaration of Independence," "The Surrender of Burgoyne," "Surrender of Lord Cornwallis," "The Resignation of Washington," "The Embarkation of the Pilgrims," and "The Landing of Columbus." The pictures are fair examples of high class art, and any one visiting the Capitol is sure to see them, as they are in the Rotunda or chief vestibule entrance. In the lobbies of the Senate Chamber and Hall of Representatives are statues of Washington and other eminent American senators and representatives. The door at the entrance of main portico is composed of bronze, and was made in Munich. It must be several tons, and is a work of rare merit. There are eight or ten panels, and every panel has a subject connected with the early history of the land, such as the incidents of Columbus's life connected with his enterprises of discovery; some of the crowned heads who figured in relation to it; and the same in reference to Cabot. The whole surface of it is bristling with subjects and objects of interest and beauty. By the same artist that painted the frescoes on the canopy of the Rotunda, there is a fresco in the staircase leading to the Hall of Representatives, styled "Western Emigration," the finest picture in the Capitol. There are also pictures in the other staircases, such as "The Battle of Lake Erie" between the British and Americans, and there are pictures of battles between the States and Mexico. These are incentives in the way of stirring up the martial spirit in "Young America,"

and likely to make him take a pride and interest in
such matters.

It is scarcely possible to notice all that is of worth,
merit, or beauty. In this great pile there are stair
cases and lobbies of beautiful white and variegated
marbles, having colonnades and corridors of the same
materials, and articles of value with rich carved and
sculpture work. The rooms of the higher legislative
functionaries are richly furnished and decorated with
representative emblems of the departments—there
are busts, portraits and statues of leading men
profusely added to the furniture of the department.
The Bureau of the Agricultural Department was at
one time in the Capitol but is removed to a building
used for that purpose alone. In this apartment where
they used to meet are various frescoes telling the
part which Americans have played in relation to that
art. Mural decorations are profuse, and a pictorial
parallel in the lives of Washington and Cincinnatus
of being called from the plough to the sword. This
room is a complete banquet of floral art fragrant to
the most sensitive nerve, and is the work of the
American-Italian Brumidi. The other rooms, especially those on the principal floors of the north
wing surrounding the Senate Chamber are beautifully
finished in every department of highest art. The
Senate Chamber is 112 feet long, 82 feet in breadth,
and 36 feet high. The galleries accommodate about

1,000 persons. The seats for the Senators are all arranged round the chair of the President in a semi-circle in three rows, and there are seventy in all. There is provision for 27 reporters of newspapers in the House, but somewhere about 46 manage to represent themselves here, of which some six or eight are local, the others being from other States. The Hall of Representatives is 130 feet long, 93 feet in breadth, and 30 feet high, and is arranged in the same manner as the Senate Hall, but the circle is twice the depth of that in the other House, for the number of representatives is 240. The galleries are not so deep in this hall, but are longer, and possibly seat as many as the gallery of the Senate. There is provision for 47 reporters in this gallery, but an addition of 15 manage to get in. There is a library in the back part of the centre building, but it is not of any extent. It was burned at the attack by the British in 1814, and suffered an accidental fire in 1861. The crypt of the Capitol is worthy of notice. The basement storey in the centre, under the Rotunda, is supported by quite an array of pillars, giving evidence of the great strength of the structure overhead.

To contemplate this magnificent and imposing mass of architectural beauty, robed in the silvery and luminous radiance of a moonlight night, from the Capitol grounds, when parapet, pediment, capital, architrave, cornice, column, and base are basking in a scene of rare and ghost-like glory, while the deepening shadows on the arches, porticos, and silent colonnades wrap it in a solemn sublimity of grandeur and repose. While the distant city with all its surroundings of magnificence, serves for a background of quiet, restful grey, and the Potomac ripples and sparkles like a sea of glass under the pale orb of night, and the distant hills of Virginia are mantled in broken shadows from the fleecy clouds which float slowly over them, and the gigantic dome seems to lift itself into the skies, and "Freedom," like a wary and sleepless sentinel, poised on his thousand emblems of strength and security, looks over the land with a keen and watchful eye, guarding his institution and his fame in to see a sight which will fix itself in the mind and remain while memory has a seat in the temple of the soul.

One could spend a long time among the matters of interest in and about this stupendous mansion, but I will only take a glance at a statue in the Capitol grounds. The first look you take at it from a short distance you take it for Julius Cæsar, but on nearing it you discover it is intended for a statue of General Washington, executed by the artist of "Greek Slave" notoriety. The whole contour of the figure is Roman. The attitude and disposition of the drapery are Roman. The sword and general accessories are Roman, and the attitude almost that where Metellus Cimber pulls the imperial purple from the shoulder of Julius Cæsar, and the sword of Brutus is sheathed in his heart. A queer conceit, and one wonders how the people of this great Republic should allow the sculptor to murder the great Washington in the Capitol grounds, so that his individuality is lost and his friends do not know him. The grounds around the Capitol are in a miserable condition, but as the Capitol itself is not finished, that may be a reason why they are so. The site is a most suitable and magnificent one, and in a few years, if the present temper of the Executive is kept alive, there is every reason to believe that the grounds and amenities will be worthy of the centre they encircle, for now they are widening the grounds and levelling up where it is necessary, and in other parts doing the opposite, so as to secure a wide and extensive plateau, that, when replete with the surroundings and adornments which are in contemplation, this great and chief object of admiration, and centre of attraction in the " Federal City," will then be recognised as worthy the man, the warrior, and the statesman for whom it was called Washington.

Leaving the Capitol, the next object of interest in point of importance is the building of the Treasury Department, and we notice it is on the two public sides draped in black for one of the officials in this department who died lately. The black cloth is hung from pillar to pillar, in graceful folds, with ends intervening. I dare say it is very well understood the kind of work which is carried on in this department of the Government service. There are a great number of young ladies engaged in various branches about the office. The building is a very fine one, and of very considerable interest in an architectural point. It is of marble and granite, and the grounds are tastefully laid off. It is contiguous to the White House or the Executive Mansion; and this is of great interest, being the official residence of the President of the Union. All strangers call on him, and following the stereotyped routine of civility I did so also. I thought as he was a great Celt he might have a pleasure and gratification in meeting a brother Celt, but even and it he was out of the way, and I had to put up with the disappointment; but I was bent upon seeing what kind of house the nation provides for their Chief Magistrate, and in this mood I went in by one of the windows. For the President's business I found, was in the hands of tradesmen and plasterers; renovations were going on in the upper parlour, to the left and it was filled to the roof with the necessary scaffolding for such renovations. The rooms and the corresponding one on the other side are about 30 feet by 22 feet. The hall, or, as we would call it, the vestibule is about 50 by 40. There is a larger room called the banqueting room about 80 feet by 40, and a large dining room. The other apartments about the house are very much what are to be found in any similar house; but up-stairs the President has the official bureau and the vice and assistant secretaries. The outside of the mansion is all white, and hence its name, I presume; and the feeling generally is abroad that it is marble. However, that is not the case, and any one seeing it must consider it is not at all like what the Presidential mansion ought to be; but the Americans have their own ideas on this point, and so far as we have been able to translate them, they do not accord with the breadth and bulk of their sentiments on other matters. Previous to the year that the seat of Government was removed to Washington, the Chief Magistrate of the States had no official house. They may have been poor at the time of starting life in the line of self-government, and their aspirations were modified commensurably with their pretensions, which any person of experience must see was wisely designed. I have no doubt when John Adams went into it in 1800 he would consider it a very magnificent and courtly palace; and I doubt not the goodwife would be somewhat perplexed in regard to how she was to govern her domestics and manage the imposing array of duties which would naturally fall to her lot to perform.

The exterior of the mansion and its surroundings of arborial and floral garniture, and the extent of the grounds, are of a medium quality, and exact no expression of an adulatory kind; but perhaps these may

share the attention of the gentlemen who has the
matter entrusted to his care, and I doubt not now
that the neighbourhood is being adorned with the
beautiful and massive group of masonry devoted to
the departments of State, that a general adjustment
of these inequalities will be the result. The grounds
are certainly far too limited for the Saturday afternoon of fashion concerts; but what they want in amplitude they have in adaptation, for the miniature halls
here and there are serviceable during the performances
of the band, and I believe the grounds will be
additionally crowded when the President's new mansion
is occupied, for I suppose in this particular the
people of Washington are the same as the people at
home here, more disposed to turn out when such is
the case. This part of the city will be a thriving
locality when the extensive granite buildings close
by are finished and the army, navy and state departments take possession with their crowds of officials.

The next building is the Patent Office. This is
the institution where one can form a capital idea of
the home, circumstance and taste of the people
among whom he is sojourning. There are some
things here which do not claim relation to the
mechanisms, but are heirlooms of the nation and
curiosities, and would be more appropriate in a
museum. Unless it is the intention that there should
be a portion of the building reserved for that purpose

indicated by their presence. There are models of works of art, buildings, and in one case are relics of the man who holds the first place in the affections of the nation, and relics and mementos of him are seen everywhere; however, those which are conserved here are his military trappings, and the utensils of his tent or camp, but the greatest wonders are his armorial bearings. These are relics of an old country, old relations, and things forgotten in the dim and distant past; but there they are, and show the chain of evidence of his being a scion of an old and powerful family, even of the race of kingmakers, the Earls of Warwick. But he should have no lineage, for the Americans would claim for him the likeness of Melchisedec of old, and of being virtually the first man. They won't allow even Adam's claim, for they say, "Well if you talk of foreigners, that may be ; but I guess George Washington was the first man who was not a foreigner." I think it is very evident, from looking at these same armorial bearings, which are in this case among the relics of Washington, that the stars and stripes are taken from them, for it is noticeable that the nucleus of the flag is traceable in it, in the fact that stars are there, and the bars by being elongated would produce a very near approach to the American flag. That may or may not be its origin, but it looks to me to be something like it. If it is so, the flag has been imported from the Old

Country, and its reconstruction only the work of the
New

The building is very capacious and elegant, and in
looking around one can form a tolerably accurate
estimate of the intense activity of the inventive brain
of the country. It is not possible to detail to any
extent the number or the character of the various
inventions which have been sent in by applicants
for patents. Their name is legion. Perhaps the
best way will be to submit the details of the same
for the last year. The Commissioner of Patents
reports to the Secretary of the Interior, in whose
department this falls to be noticed, that there were
20,354 applications filed at the Patent Office, 283
applications for extension of patents, and 519 applications for registration of trade marks; nearly 13,000
patents, including reissues and designs, were issued
and 235 extended, and 965 allowed but not issued
by reason of non-payment of final fees. 3,274 caveats
were filed, and 475 trade marks registered. The fees
received during the same period from all sources
amounted to 70,162,672 dols., and the total expenditure to 60,944,960 dols., making the receipts 2,177
dols. in excess of the expenditure. The Government
appropriate various amounts for the encouragement
of the inventions, and drawings and details are
published and printed at the Government Printing
Office, and by these means the inventive genius of

the people is induced and fostered. Although it is implied, it may be as well for me to state, that in this office there are models of all the inventions kept which have been allowed or accepted by the examiners; and there is quite a collection, as may be assumed from the number which has passed during the year just ended. The space is great, but it is found it will be necessary to increase it at an early date. The building, as it stands at present, has evidently been built at different periods, and is a massive pile of masonry.

The next building in the Government connection is the Agricultural Department. This was in the Capitol formerly, but now there is a fanciful and appropriate building devoted to this business of the Executive. The various officials have offices in the main and upper storeys, and there is a museum in the centre of the upper storey, and Professor Townend Glover very courteously explained the object that was contemplated by the classification which he was carrying out, which seemed to be based on quite an enlightened and scientific principle. Any one of the agricultural products specified by us, the Professor showed us where it was a native of, and what parts of the country were best suited for its propagation, and the kind of insects which were most destructive to that product. There were all the products of the various States connected with this art. In one office

obelisk at present looks at a distance like an immense sugarhouse chimney whitewashed, but when you near it you discover it to be composed of white marble, and you feel that ultimately something very grand will emanate from what is at present conspicuously crude and unseemly. I presume that the Government must have charge of what is chargeable in relation to its condition, and if it is in the hands of Government officials it is not to be wondered that it is subject to intervals of stagnation, for in America a change of Government is at times the cause of disastrous and evil consequences, as it affects all the various ramifications of the Executive down to the public scavenger. But it is pleasing to notice in connection with this matter that the people are not behind, for there are stored close by a great number of donations for this paralysed public work—gifts which represent all the prosperous provident and beneficent institutions in the country, such as Freemasons, Oddfellows, Foresters, Firemen, and many kindred societies—these are chiefly in the form of large blocks of marble, and on them are the emblems of the craft, and mottoes, or the order represented, some of them beautifully cut, and must have been forwarded there at great expense, and it must be very annoying to the donors to have them shut up and wasting their beauty in the desert air.

Not far from this is another building called the

headed by the President of the Union, and we in charity suppose that it is well managed at least. But one cannot help thinking how much wiser, how much more beneficent, would it have been on the part of the donor to have set agoing and completed such a liberal work during his lifetime, rather than have it fall short, and be blurred and curtailed by the acts of trustees or regents, who at times look more to their own emoluments than the object for which it was founded, or the posthumous fame of the donor.

The Navy Yard is reckoned a point of interest, and is situated at a distance south of the city. This branch of industry connected with the Executive of the States is not confined altogether to the Capital. Philadelphia and New York share in this enterprise, and these places are better adapted for it than the shores of the Potomac. There is, or was, a quiet and unenterprising look about the whole works. There was not a craft of any size or pretentions in or near the docks or slips, save one steamer, which, I think, was engaged in some of the minor or subordinate services, such as the transporting of heavy materials. There were lots of cannons, mortars, shells, and other kinds of engines that are used for purposes of war; and while I was determined to discover if there really was something worthy of being seen, the fire bells were rung in such a manner that they might be heard as far as Chesapeake Bay, and in an instant

about five or six hundred men with all the newest
appliances for fire extinguishing, and with steam-
engine churning and any number of hatchets, ladders,
buckets, coils and officers, fifers, drummer, and bugler,
rushed like an army of locusts to a particular spot,
and began to fire away on the large wooden shed
which contained the building-yard, and which was
about eighty feet high, and the steam-engine sent the
water over the shed easily. Then after they had
thoroughly soaked the whole for a short time the
bugler sounded the "retreat" or "cease firing" and
the steam business was at an end. These fire drills
take place every now and again and qualify the
workmen to operate on fires with great rapidity. I
think about seven minutes served to put the engine
at full steam and at times it looked as if it would
leap off the ground.

There are some very fine churches in this city, and
the church-going Americans devote much care, time
and money to them. I accompanied a gentleman to
the church where Mr U. S. Grant the President, etc.
expecting to see him there; as I failed to do so at
the time, I called at the Executive Mansion, but I
was doomed to disappointment for a second time,
but there were greater losses at "Bunker's Hill" and
I thought no more about it. The manner of conducting services was the same as in the Rev. Mr

Beecher's; a subordinate did the subordinate or minor duties, and the person who preached did that duty only. It was not the pastor of the church, for he was in Europe at the time, and a notice was read that he had sailed from Britain homewards, and might be expected on the following Sunday. Nearly all the clergymen in the well-to-do churches in the cities were on the Continent of Europe this year, and on the other side I saw many who were doing the States from Europe.

The population of Washington is about double that of Greenock. There are some sixty-two churches, which is double that of this town. There are no manufactures of any kind carried on, and the Navy Yard is the only public work in the place. The better class of dwelling-houses are built with brick and stone, but there are many, very many, of the houses built with wood, and these houses change their sites easily, when any occasion demands such a change; and they very often lift a brick house and build a storey below, and thus pursue the opposite tack to that of builders in this country. I saw a public market at Georgetown which was lifted up in this way, and there was not a crack in the plaster-work in the inside when it was completed. The building would be fifty or sixty feet long, and twenty-five or so broad. There is a large proportion of the

population black, but I will refer to this new element
of American citizenship again when I see a little
more of it and in the meantime I will take the cars
in the direction of the old capital and Baltimore and
take farewell of the "Federal City."

CHAPTER VII.

BALTIMORE.

AFTER a run of two hours or so we arrived at Baltimore. It was near midnight, and the place, so far as one could see, for there was only enough of light in the streets to make darkness visible, was not possessed of features strikingly charming; and the contrast between this place and Washington was enhanced by the great disparity in the width of the streets, which could be easily noticed even in the dark; and after coursing along a number of them, I was set down at the end of a street, which was the nearest point to my hotel—"The Fountain," I think it was called—and after crossing two blocks I was at the end of my journey for the day. As it was even too late for making enquiries regarding the succeeding day's operations, I consigned myself, a solitary fraction, to the great company who were "a' noddin'" in the quarters around. There was a considerable difference in the quality of my dormitory from the last, but one of my friends who directed my steps to this place was responsible for that, and as my programme would not allow me to tabernacle for any length of time here, it did not matter much. So

having extinguished the "light of other days," which
was carried from the down stairs portion of the hotel
I wrapt myself in the scanty coverings of my couch
and waited for the morning. I had put into a room
in the back part of the hotel and when morning
dawned I was regaled with a succession of "vocal
notes wild." There must have been a flock of all
kinds of birds and beasts, and if I had been within a
reasonable distance of Chanticleer I would have
changed his tune and destroyed the discordant
medley which was being discoursed in the back yard
to my disgust and annoyance. So I thought the
best thing I could do was to walk abroad and see the
strange surroundings and besides if such were in
the place I would be obliged to spend one day at
least.

When I began my work of inspection I found my
hotel was located in what I thought the oldest, and
judged the most crowded part of the city and I was
anxious to seek for some more open and modern
locality. So I started off, but in my progress I found
useless to expect to realize a wise expert but I discovered my route was in the direction of the harbour
and the harbour I presumed in the course the be
likelihood was there of my success. as I kept
my course along a street which had a considerable
incline, as I was anxious to gain some elevated position where I could see at a glance the configuration

of the land, and the extent to which it was peopled; and learning that there was close by a monument of Washington, I sought it out and at once began my perilous ascent. I have been on many such heights, but the task of scaling this monument has cured me of trying any like enterprise again, for in the staircase, from top to bottom, there is not a single opening for the admission of air or light, and one has to cheer his path with the solitary rays of an oil lamp, and the resident odours left by former excelsiors, engaged on the same mission, were calculated to stifle all one's aspirations to get up in that part of the world. But when once up—the object once attained, and attained by labour at times threatening to exhaust your energies—you feel that the enjoyment is enhanced in proportion. From this point the whole country lies open to the circuit of your gaze: the sloping hills beginning to clothe themselves in the variegated tints of autumn; the Paptapsco reflecting the broad glare of the morning sun, and dotted with its coasting fleet of steam and sailing vessels, and the busy harbour, its chequered housetops, its spires, its minarets, and cathedral dome with gilded cross, its public marts, hotels, and banking houses, densely packed in squares and solid blocks. The streets are all narrow and long, and the houses in the principal streets very high, having the effect of making them look narrower than they really are. There are some fine shops and several magnificent hotels, but the narrow dirty streets detract from every object that comes in contact or juxtaposition with them. There is much bustle and commercial activity in the business parts of the city. The harbours are crowded, and unloading, and every sign of prosperity and industry. But one cannot see the solidity about any of the docks or buildings which characterises such structures in our ports. At home, they have plenty of granite but they seem to prefer piles of wood to piles of stone work for such purposes, and they have a very superficial and dirty appearance.

The streets in Baltimore are a study of themselves. It must be one of those cities, the modern cities in which I was kept close to the type of the streets to in the Old World where ground is usually dear, for I don't remember seeing one sufficiently broad to run two lines of tramway rails on, and the city seems to be built on a succession of hills of no great dimensions, which give it a peculiar look. In the lower parts of the city the drains must be quite inadequate for their functions at times, for the curbstones are nearly a foot high and at some places a row of stepping stones is laid across from one side of the street to the other to enable one to pass when floods take possession of the streets; or it may be the case that they have not introduced the underground common sewer, but just allow the streets themselves to carry off the drainage, and make them serve instead, and in that case they will have ample ventilation for these common sewers, and will be exempt from that perplexing question.

Close by the Washington monument are some very fine buildings, and some of the wealthiest citizens live in this locality. Here, is a building resembling a city hall, a present to the citizens of Baltimore by Mr Peabody, and is worthy of the donor. There, is a splendid lecture-hall, elegantly fitted up, and commodious rostrum and retiring rooms, and there is also a free library, containing 50,000 volumes. It is, I believe, next in extent to the library in the Capitol, which they are pleased to call a public library, but it is not a free library, and numbers 180,000 volumes, and includes the library of the Supreme Court as well.

The only sight which deserves commendation in Baltimore is the fine public park, which is called the "Druids' Park." It is out on the outskirts of the city, and the tramway cars run into the centre of it, but not by the principal entrance. Visitors going in by the side are apt to miss the sight of the main entrance. At it there is a fine gateway of stone, but not elaborately ornamented, rather a common-looking one, and when you pass through you get a glimpse of the extent and character of the grounds, which are seven hundred acres in extent, beautifully wooded,

and furnished with every requirement of a public
park. Along the sides of the principal walks at
entering are forty immense vases, raised on pedestals,
in all about twelve feet high, and the vases are filled
with Indian cress and other kinds of creepers, which
fall down over the pedestal, and slope across the
banks of the side walks. At one turn you are
coursing along the banks of an extensive lake, with
small parties of pleasure-seekers in boats engaged in
a hunt after the birds which are skimming the
waters; and at another you are threading your way
through a maze of tall trees, forming one continuous
high arborial arch, under which you cool and regale
yourself to fit you for fresh discoveries by woods and
groves. And, anon, you enter a labyrinth with
figures hedged in on all sides, with high and fragrant
walls, and under foot a *carpet vert* of rich and heavy
foliage whose meshes are vocal with swarms of busy
alatoria, which sparkle in the sun as you tread
your way over their dwellings; and then some curi-
ously-constructed Chinese temple is passed, rich in
variety of bright colours, and grotesque and beautiful
form; a temple of Apollo, around which thousands
are wont on holidays to crowd, and let the sweet
sounds of music creep into their ears and bask in the
fragrance of the generous *zephyrs* as they come
loaded with the sweets from this lovely garden of
Nature. The walks take you by quiet retreats where

you can while away the day in dreamy solitude; or by the clusters of juveniles, showily clad in Oriental style, and busy at croquet or other pastimes; or through the covered sylvan paths ornamented with rockery, rustic bridges and chairs; or by the fountains with their shoals of shiny and tiny fishes, sparkling like fireflies in the trembling and crystal flakes from the *jet d'eau* above. After ascending to the balcony over the refreshment rooms, where a good view of the park, with its lakes, streams, waterfalls, gardens, and temples is got, you take the car, which comes close up to this point, leaving by the side gates or entrances, where another car is found to take you to the city. And now the city, which was formerly an object of little attraction, has become an object you feel disposed to avoid after seeing the fairy garden of the "Druids' Park," so your thoughts are of having your baggage checked and taking the road for the ancient capital. With this outline of proceeding roughly sketched the hotel is reached, and our slender liabilities adjusted, we seek the cars, get once more upon the line, and feel some satisfaction of having seen, and more of having left, one of the dirtiest cities in the Union.

As usual, we are taken along a succession of streets, preceded with the music of the great bell on the engine, and shortly we are steaming over bridges and swamps in the direction of Pennsylvania. We pass

Aberdeen, and by-and-bye we halt, and in an instant
the car, which before was almost empty, is filled to
suffocation with the sons and daughters of slaves,
and the little light which the dainty globes before
afforded is totally absorbed by this new importation.
I had heard of these savages attacking white men
partly for mere amusement, and if any such disposition should be evinced by this lot, the chances were
all in favour of "black;" but we learned that these
were "good niggers," and we were disposed to look
on them in not such a "dark light." I say we
learned, and our information was to the effect that
they were just returned from a camp meeting which
I believe outheroils Herod in some of its features.
When some of the darkies get inspired their exclama-
tions and declamations are vivid and very sparkling
This one could believe for their volubility was something surpassing the conception of a person of medium
calibre. Perhaps it would be too much to say that
it was language without saying it was language of a
kind, of that kind we sometimes call "jargon"—a
sort of chattering with an element of sense in it
Much din and little else, but the oft repeated sample
of something like "tony," "caes," and "dolfy," made
us feel we were in the company of distinguished
individuals and we could not help thinking that in
all likelihood we were in the presence of Mark
Antony, Julius Cæsar, and Gustavus Adolphus and

we began to look round to see if the fair descendant of the Ptolemies was not among the crew; but the light was insufficient to enable us to discover any element which could ally itself with the *personnel* of that fair Egyptian, and we gave it up, and were beginning to look at their traits of character in connection with some of the aspects of natural philosophy submitted by Smillie, Lord Monboddo, and Darwin, when the train stopped, and as by that uniformity of instinct which is an ingredient in the constitution of some of the creatures which herd together, they disappeared in a mass. This had the effect of disposing us more thoroughly for a course of contemplative thought, which is attended in its action with an indefinite number of "whys" and "hows." We thought that in the war of races the preservation of the negro race was a miracle, and yet it was not so. It certainly was so in a country where a bold, hardy, generous and warlike race like the aborigines of the land had disappeared before the progress of civilisation which accompanied the march of the white man into the interior of his former abode; and there we have the negro full in the enjoyment of civil and political freedom and privileges, while the other suffers extirpation and death. And if we ask how or why it is for a lifetime, we could but receive one answer, and that is, because he was a slave. And that answer involves a thousand facts.

The most prominent one is, as a nation they are unfit to take care of themselves. And when President Lincoln delivered his notable speech in the Senate, and when the nation accepted the responsibility of giving the nigger his freedom, they thought not that they had rough-hewn to themselves a problem on the facade of the great fabric of their constitution which would task all their legislative wisdom and their administrative acumen and dexterity to finish the details and make them acceptable to the diverse elements which constitute their Republic. Of course it would be too much to expect the same generation to denounce its own act seeing there is so much to cause them to do the opposite, or even to admit that they had committed a mistake, which I have no doubt many think now although they are not ready to say so. On the principle that everything is fair in war the North fulminates an edict in which they declare the servants of the slave-owning States free, with the view of embarrassing the action of the South in the battle-field and perpetrating an act of robbery under the guise of a supposed right of government, and thereby reducing many in the South to a state bordering on beggary, through the loss of their property, and no compensation is thought of or given to those who have lost their whole, and who had their slaves disposed of under the plea that they were rebels and ought to be thankful of to any left an the possession of their own heads. How different was the case of our own country. When we wanted to get quit of the stain connected with the guilt associated with the trade, we bargained with the owner and paid him the commercial value, and set the negroes free. But the Yankee in his 'cuteness conceived his purchase would be too dear at any money value, and he adopted the least expensive, by making it a necessity of the dispute, though it was not primarily an element in it, for at the same time the political value of a coloured citizen was reckoned in the statute book at three-fifths that of a white man.

It has been said that history repeats itself. We have seen that the Americans have in many instances associated themselves in idea with the early Republics. The Lacedæmonians, like them, had their helots, and they at one time affected to confer rights on them, which they found afterwards ill-accorded with the name and prestige of these heroic Spartans, and almost as soon as they were invested were they divested of them, for reasons much the same as are found in America to-day, and these chiefly by the importance with which they have become inflated in connection with their electoral power. The niggers are favoured and courted for their vote, and promises made to them which inspire them with ideas of being senators and members of Congress; but their *E pluribus unum* does not read in that way, and it is a ques-

tion, if ever they will allow it to do so. They are
not the children of the land which might have
weight if they were so in securing perpetual immuni-
ties to them; but they are not and their labour is
irregular and unavailable, their conduct is brutish,
and there are frequently contests, arising out of
nothing but the question of colour, which end in
bloodshed, and most like will end some day in the
extinction of the race, so far as America is concerned.
The Americans are a hard working people, and they
and the blacks are ill-paired in this particular, at
the intervals at which the one has a newspaper, while
the other, like a pig, is snoring his precious time
away under the burning rays of the sun, and he
looks quite at home in that condition, anything but
work. And he is sure to be found in a variety of
enterprises where the easiest kind of labour is wanted.
They are found in bands perambulating the country
and delineating the felicity of their condition when
living upon the plantation in the South, and sometimes on a roving excursion to other lands, singing
a kind of spiritual comic songs, but always in charge
of some pale face, for it is an indispensable feature
in their social economy to have some such one to
take them in charge. This may be to them a difficulty they often experience—that of being denied
admittance to railway cars, &c. which looks like a
hardship, but goes to show that the black nuisance

of Republicanism is not relished, and will be dispensed with by those arbitrary masters who are shut up from taking any action till the facts of the late rebellion are partially forgotten. But the lamps of the old capital are beginning to flicker in the distance, and the waters of the Delaware are reflecting the lights on the many wharves on the curve of the river, and the dim outlines of the Quaker City are getting stronger and stronger, the lights brighter and brighter, and the big bell rings out its warning voice, and shortly the train is at rest, and crowds are getting on the tramway cars, and following the example of "the lave," we mount, and set off for our hotel after our ride from Baltimore.

CHAPTER VIII

PHILADELPHIA

If the historian, the antiquarian, or the philologist were in quest of a field for enterprising labour, I think the ancient capital of the Union would be about the best that he could select; for I think no modern city is equal to their wants in the way of furnishing the amount of materials. In point of historic interest the old capital of the Union will always hold a firm place, for there is much connected with the history of it which will always secure for it a prominent place among the cities of the Union. When we come to institute inquiries, our interrogations are met by a string of replies almost too numerous to transfer to the memory, and to retain them there. One name is so closely associated with this track of country that one instinctively wishes to know how the agent, the Quaker, is so prominently before you wherever you go; and as the incidents explanatory of this are worthy of being recited, it may be as well to state that that portion of America called the State of Pennsylvania was handed over to the Penn family in, or as payment of, a debt by Charles the Second, in the exercise of the "Right Divine" he so scrupulously contended for, and William Penn, a hundred and ninety years ago went out to take possession of it, which he did; planned a city on what he considered the most advantageous spot, constructed a code, and appointed an executive in conjunction with himself for the conduct of civil affairs.

But during this time there was one important and striking transaction which fell to be consummated. The land, though sold by the King to Admiral Penn, was possessed by the aborigines of the country, and Penn had to treat with these people, so as to let him have undisturbed possession, and this negotiation has its record preserved on a stone called "The Penn Treaty Monument," which is inscribed with the words, "Treaty Ground of William Penn and the Indian Nation, 1682," and concludes with the words, "Unbroken Faith." We may ask why so many of the subsequent treaties between the Indian and American cannot have the "Unbroken Faith" added to them?

In the name of the State itself we discover much that is indicative of the kind of land Penn found when he landed in the "blue anchor." About a year before the occasion which I refer to, the name, which is something akin to the term "Penn's Garden," at once brings up a land of forests, and this is fully borne out in the name of the streets, which, I believe, were so named; and so far as we can judge there

must have been quite a variety in that part of the
country. The streets generally run at right angles.
Those running from east to west have names and
those running across are by numbers, and on a fine
principle, for instance, from Front to First Street ex-
hausts the first 100, and at Second Street begins 200,
the odd numbers on one side, the even numbers on
the other, and it matters not whether the whole
numbers between the hundreds are exhausted or not,
the Third, Fourth, or Fifth Streets begin the fourth
or fifth hundred, as the case may be, and by this
arrangement, if one knows the number sought you
can go to the nearest point to it from any part of
the city by car or foot, and as the cars have the
names of streets on them through which they run,
the city is easily overtaken. The streets which are
main arteries of the city are named Alden, Aspen,
Almond, Beach, Cedar, Cherry, Chesnut, Elm, Fil-
bert, Jessamine, Linden, Myrtle, Olive, Pine, Poplar,
Sycamore, Spruce, Vine, Walnut, Willow, and one
can see from these variety was not awanting and you
can see as great a variety as you like in the condition
of the streets. The causeway of the great majority
of the streets is very inferior to our own but is similar to the streets in other towns and cities in the
Union; but there are some of the finest pavements
on the chief streets I ever saw, composed of granite,
containing from 70 to 80 cubic feet of rough dressed

flags and the curb of the same material; generally there is but one car on the narrow street, and the cars on that street all run in the same direction, and if you want to go in the opposite you must go to the next block, and you will find the same cars going the opposite way. On many of the streets, though comparatively narrow, there are trees planted along their entire length, which give them a handsome appearance; but when a fine building is on one of these its attractiveness suffers very much, and very many of the best buildings in the city are so placed; but the finest buildings are all on open spaces, and there are very many of these, but some of the buildings whose outsides are not very attractive, are very interesting on account of their historical connections and associations. They will point out to you the house where the first American flag was made; the house that stands where Penn landed, where his own house stood, which only lately disappeared; the church where he worshipped; and the first house of Parliament, the old " Carpenter's Hall," and " Independence Hall," the hall where the " Continental Congress " held its first sitting on the day after the bombardment of Boston took place by the troops of the King of Great Britain and Ireland, and where declaration of independence was made, and which was subsequently used by the British troops as barracks, and was afterwards used as a bank, but is now used to hold the "memories of the past" in the form of anything which is a memento of those stirring times or of men who played a part in the great scenes of the nation's liberty from the galling yoke of British bondage, a considerable number of portraits of American warriors and statesmen, from Washington to Lincoln. The old bell which rang out a merry peal at the time of the declaration of Independence on the 4th of July, 1776, is consigned among the relics of those Gory times. There is a hall upstairs, and in this hall Washington delivered his farewell address, when he left the sword to return to the plough, like the Greek and Roman heroes of old. On the top of this building there is a spire but I never aspired to mount any height other Washington column at Baltimore. Off this one, it is said, you can get a good view of the city but I doubt it, as it is no height, and so far as I could learn, there was no elevation in Philadelphia where there is access to view the land at least of that kind. Opposite this building, on the pavement, is a statue of Washington encircled with a rail of iron, for this is the most public place in the city. The General Post Office is close by but it is unworthy of a remark, but a new one is in course of erection and if I remember me was the third or fourth instance of a like kind I had noticed in the cities of the Union and they are all magnificent buildings. Another monument of the early days of the Union is the grave of the Philosopher Franklin, in a modest, homely spot by the public highway. With nothing but the iron fencing of the churchyard between, can be seen the grave of Franklin and his wife, as they repose beneath the shadow of the overhanging branches of a tree, and a large stone slab reveals to the traveller the resting-place of the great citizen of the world.

In this city there are some finer buildings than are to be seen out of the capital. There are several newspaper offices that equal the *Herald* office in New York, and the leading businesses in the city have warehouses and offices which are examples of architecture, and stand very high, if they can be excelled anywhere. The banks, hotels, and theatres, of which there are six; museums, libraries, and scientific institutions, colleges and churches, benevolent institutions, cemeteries, and public parks. There is a library for the use of apprentices, and a school of design for women. There are hospitals and asylums, mints, arsenals, docks, navy yards, sugar refineries, shipbuilding yards. It is not possible to refer to but a few, and I will take a college for the first, as the donor, from the extent of his benefaction, is entitled to precedence. The college is called after the donor, " Girard College," which, with its surroundings, is built on forty-five acres, and cost 200,000 dollars in construction. The building is of white marble, and

said to be finest specimen of Grecian architecture in
America. It is much like the temple of Diana at
Ephesus or at Magnesia, or the temple of Virtue and
Honour at Rome, or rather like the latter as the
colonnade is a single row of columns, whereas the
two former had double colonnades. The pediment is
plain, there is no figure design of any kind in the
recess, there is only a single medillion on the cornice,
and no enrichment on the freize, there is only a
single door on the facade, and the steps are continued
round the whole building. In the vestibule there is
a statue of the donor in white marble and he looks a
heavenly and eccentric person, as I believe he was.
The funds at the disposal of the trustees of the col
lege enable them to educate about five hundred
orphans, from the white population only aged from
six to ten years, and they are clothed, fed and
educated until they are eighteen years of age when
they must leave. In the wards of the college are
libraries and museums, where specimens of the work
of the students are seen, class rooms and lecture halls;
and in an apartment on the top floor are seen the
relics of the donor's household — old fashioned book
stand, chairs, tables, pictures, and a variety of such
things as were found in houses in the world, when
men did not spend all their means to deck things as
were calculated to astonish their neighbours but
could save something for such purposes like old

Stephen Girard. On the top of this college a fine view of the country is got, and we observe that the college is laid on the roof with tiles of white marble, and the gross weight of what covers the roof is within a fraction of 1,000 tons. Round the main buildings are the residences of the students, and the grounds are laid out in a tasteful manner; and in the yard is a monument raised to a number of the students who fell in the war between the North and South. It is like a little temple supported on four pillars, and inside is a statue of a volunteer, fully equipped, and on a pannel are the names of the young men who fell, and the battles they were engaged in. There are splendid walks and drives in the park, and the whole is enclosed with massive walls. Such is one of the benefactions of Stephen Girard. The second is in the very heart and centre of the busiest part of the city, where several acres of land which belonged to him have been built upon, and the ground rents go by virtue of his settlement to lessen the taxation of the city; and some of his estates, which have improved since he died, will, I presume, be devoted to increase these benefactions or create others. There are several buildings which one can also mention so as to give an idea of the quality of the city, but to describe would require a volume to do so satisfactorily. The first I will mention is the Horticultural Hall, which, I believe, was the first of

the kind in the country. The style of the building
is what I would be inclined to call Grecian route,
and is a massive, handsome building. I believe
when their floral and pomological displays take
place, they can fill the immense auditorium to suffocation. Close by is the Academy of Music, the
largest opera-house in the United States. The building is an elegant one, in the Italian type of the Byzantine school. The hall is nearly 200 by 200 and
70 feet high, and will seat nearly 3,000 persons.
Then again, there is the Academy of Natural
Science, an ample-looking building in the style of
Gothic architecture, with all the various class rooms,
lecture room, and others. The library contains about
23,000 volumes, and the museum about 250,000 specimens in the departments of zoology, geology and
botany, and 65,000 of mineral fossils. The botanical
collection is said to be exceeded only by the collection in the British Museum, and the collection of
birds is both rich and attractive.

I was desirous to know over if there was any Fine Art
collection in the city, but I was told that that department
ments of art was in a state of transitory state, the old
Fine Art gallery was defunct, and the new one was
unfinished, so the pictures could not be seen. I
don't know what that meant, but I was unsuccessful
in seeing any pictures anywhere in the States. The
new building could not be seen except on the plans.

but it will be worthy of the city when completed, and the next time I go back I will probably be more successful in the Fine Art line; but it is likely if I had seen that I would not have seen something else, for where there is so much to see, and one's time limited, that must of necessity be the case.

One of the three mints which produce the circulating medium of the States is here in one of the chief streets of the city, and is an object of attraction; but as the engraver and the printer have been chiefly engaged on the American money for a number of years, the mint was scarcely of as much interest as it would have been had the opposite been the case. I did not see them engaged on any kind of the present metallic currency, but preparing sheets of metal for the dies. There is a museum upstairs, and in it the coins of every country in the globe are to be seen. The building itself is not a large one. It resembles a church, looking at it from the front, but when one sees the immense tall chimney standing up through the centre of it, your idea of an ecclesiastical structure evaporates in the smoke. The front of it stands close to the line of street, and is surrounded with a rail.

There is a magnificent cathedral church in one of the streets, and it is a building of considerable merit and grandeur. The dome rises over 200 feet high, and is surmounted with a large gilded cross. It is cruciform, and the style is a mixture of the Greek and Roman. In the inside are gorgeous religious accessories, and there are frescoes by Signor C Brumidi, who painted the frescoes in the Capitol at Washington, and it is designated the Cathedral of St. Peter and St. Paul. In the outskirts of the city there is a college or seminary called after St Charles Borromeo. Methinks I hear some one say, Who is he? St. Peter we know, and St Paul we know, but who is St Charles Borromeo? I thought myself I had fallen in with him somewhere before, either in the Cathedral of Milan or the Basilica Ambrosiana in that same city—a gentleman evidently of precious and eminent qualities, for all that can or could be conserved of him - namely, the bones - are to be found in one of the places named, robed in the rarest and costliest costume, composed of gold and silver, with chains, rings and crozier studded with brilliants and precious gems, and enshrined or encased in a crystal casket; and to this half-human half-artificial idol do thousands in Italy bow the knee and pour out the streams of their devotional ignorance before the skeleton of this fictitious saint. I would not have made this deviation had I not been impressed with the idea that there are very many who have never heard of St Carlo Borromeo. And one can see the estimate of his worth as accepted by the people who erected this fine seminary. It is in the Italian style, and must have cost a large sum of money. I hope the influence of the teaching by the students who are reared here will do more for America than they have done for Italy.

The villas of the merchant princes of Philadelphia are beautiful specimens of architecture. This was the only place where I saw one of these composed of white marble, and when set off on a background of fine trees and well-disposed shrubbery, had a sparkling effect in the mellow light of a summer evening. Here, as in the other large American cities, there is a public park, and they say it is the largest in the States; but for beauty and effect they are disposed to place the Central Park in New York before it The public park in Philadelphia, or Fairmount, as it is called, has the advantage of any park that I saw, for the river Schuylkill and one of its tributaries are in part enclosed in the grounds of the park, which make it one of the nearest approaches to a fairy scene which can be found anywhere. In the park are found large squares or openings, and in their centres are found monuments of notable statesmen and citizens, and these rare and incomparable works of art are fenced in with varied and skilfully arranged works of arborial and floricultural art. The river is spanned with light and airy-looking bridges, consonant with all that is seen about. Boat-houses, refreshment cafés, open drives along the banks of the Wissahickon—all

richly wooded with tall patriarchal-looking pines, and
replete with natural beauties and enhanced with the
various works of art which are usual in these places.
There are many cemeteries in and around the city.
Some of them have a mixed proprietary—others belong to lodges, such as Oddfellows—and others to
trades, such as engineers, but these are marked by
the absence of those rich works which we see in some
of the others. In Woodbine Cemetery there is a
mausoleum in the form of a Greek temple, surrounded
with a parapet, and it is allowed to be the finest of
that character in the country. One can see an isolated building of rare beauty here and there in various
places, but the finest as a whole to be seen in the
States is the Greenwood Cemetery at Brooklyn. There
is nothing can touch it anywhere out of Père la Chaise,
at Paris. The churches in Philadelphia are very
varied in styles of architecture. Some ancient, and
the modern ones are costly and reflect an amount of
credit on the members, and enrich the city in no ordinary degree. There is one built of white marble, and
recently finished, which is quite a gem. It is a Gothic
building, has a fine spire and rich tracery running
through and dividing the painted and enamel glass
windows, the light and shadow streaming across the
buttresses. The ornate and fancy work on the roof,
sparkling with its dotted burnished and irregular
fretted ridges, form a very pleasing contrast to the

monster Masonic Temple which has just been completed alongside, and which, for the benefit of the craft on this side, I will describe in my next chapter.

CHAPTER IX

MASONIC TEMPLE AT PHILADELPHIA

As I indicated formerly, there is a special interest associated with everything in this place on account of being the early capital of the Union; but apart from the interest with which we may regard Philadelphia on account of her former political position there is another which is regarded as paramount to that, for it is, so to speak, the capital of the brethren of the "mystic tie"—Freemasonry. This fact has been made doubly conspicuous lately, on account of the Masons of Pennsylvania having built an enormous temple, at the cost of somewhere about £300,000. This large building, without any other facts before one, would confirm the opinion that the number of masons was very great in and about Philadelphia. Indeed the brethren in this country have very little conception of the character of this institution in America, and especially in this city, where the brethren number 12,000 alone, and in the State somewhere about 30,000. Twenty years ago the craft completed a fine temple for their use in one of the finest sites in the city and have occupied it during that time. Six years ago it was found to be too small for their accommodation, and they resolved to build a larger one, and this building, which has just been finished and consecrated, has no equal in the world. There are 59 lodges in the city which meet in the temple, according to the various degrees, and the arrangements are such as to allow all to meet according to their degrees in Masonry. The ground on which the temple stands costs about £30,000. The site is one of the finest in the city, being at a corner of one of the principal squares, and in company with some of the finest buildings in the city. Close by this edifice they are busy putting up a block of buildings for civic purposes which measures over four hundred feet square. I think they are to be of granite. I only saw the finished drawing of them. The architect is a Scotchman, and is named Macarthur. And near to it again the Academy of Fine Arts is in course of erection; alongside of it the new Methodist Episcopal Chapel stands, which is of white marble, so that the surroundings are quite consonant with the magnificent temple of the ancient craft. The cornerstone was laid five years ago, and as a matter of course a fine display was made at the time, and the gavel which was used on the occasion was the one with which General Washington laid the cornerstone of the Capitol in Washington city. The stone itself weighed ten tons, and many valuable masonic relics were deposited in the cavity. There was a fragment of the foundation-stone from Solomon's Temple, which was dug from beneath the mosque of Omar, and a piece of marble from the golden gate of King Solomon's Temple. It also contained a piece of stone from the foundation of the temple at Jerusalem, and a piece of one of the cedars of Lebanon. This gigantic building is bounded by four streets, its length is 200 feet and 150 feet broad, and it seems to be, looking at it from the outside, three storeys high, but the tower which is the great feature of the building, is 250 feet high and rises straight from its own foundation, which is 30 feet below the line of pavement on the top, and at the angles of this tower are four turrets. On looking at these from the street they looked dwarfed but they are about 36 feet high. There is a small tower at the opposite front angle, which terminates in a sort of battlement, with four turrets, and there are numerous turrets on the central portion of the building, and one at each corner. The style of the building is Norman, and there is a breadth and massiveness about it which is imposing, and conveys an idea of stability and grandeur. The building of this temple was effected in the same manner as the Temple at Jerusalem. There was no sound of hammer or tool heard, the stones having been dressed and made ready for their places in the quarry or some place away from the city, and some but freemasons were engaged on the work during its execution. The entire façade of the building is a work of great merit and masterly architectural elaboration, defying any thing like description, especially from one whose theme is not architecture alone. The doorway or porch is singularly so. I mean the main entrance, for, like Solomon's Temple, this one has three entrances—an east, west, and south. The western is the grand entrance, and is deeply recessed to allow of ornamentation on the stonework, which is a deep and richly-carved arch of granite, with open balcony above.

Suppose we enter from the main entrance, we pass through massive and carefully constructed doors, and are ushered into the vestibule of the temple at once, and on either side are seen sphynxes, the Egyptian symbols or representations of Wisdom, Strength, and Beauty, and the fixtures for lighting the entrance are novel and curious in their construction. The main hall from this sweeps right through the building, and is laid with marble tiles in white and black, and an ornamental border surrounding the end. All along and up the stair runs a base or dado of polished marble, and the same in the lobbies, halls, and passages. The stairway is a massive iron structure, having iron railing and handrail of ebony. The steps of the stair are easy in ascending, and they are all padded with indiarubber pads, which is suggestive.

As you enter, the first symbol or figure which attracts your attention is that of Silence, which stands in the way as you seek the teaching for which the novice or candidate is in quest. A fine effect is produced on the stair and hall by having the way overhead covered with stained glass, which throws its light of varied colour on the objects below. On the upper stair hall are placed three figures in a recumbent position. These are the graces—Faith, Hope, and Charity—while the figure below stands with two fingers on her lip, indicating that to see and hear are the duties of the novice, when he ascends to higher and better teachings words are imperative. In the stained-glass window on the front side of the hall above are the various emblazonings of the various degrees of the craft, examples of rare vitreous art. On the arch are the jewels denoting the progressive steps of the fraternal labours of the craft, and representative statues of their position in Faith, Hope, Charity, Wisdom, Strength and Beauty; and below, in a circle surrounding him who was learned in all the wisdom of the Egyptian as he stands inside the learning bush, are the words in connexion with the antiquity of the Order, *Nei lux ex hac fod.*

In describing the interior of the building perhaps it would be well to take the pure Masonic order, and suiting the action to the word we must descend to the basement and come gradually to the upper parts of the temple. Down below, on a level with the foundation of the tower, there is a well of pure water, and there is an engine of eight horse-power to force up the water through the entire building; and adjacent to the various halls are eight beautiful fountains, constructed in keeping with the character of the building and of the various apartments. The pipes are so arranged in the lower depths that iced or hot water can be got to suit any occasion, and thus one of the first principles is inculcated and given effect to, on one of the fountains near the Asylum of the Knight Templars, in the words—" If any man thirst let him come unto me and drink."

I may state that the interior of the building has been so constructed that the principal halls are specimens or examples of the various schools or styles of architecture, and the furnishings, accessories, and decorations are all completed to accord with their styles. In coming up from the basement storey we are necessitated to take the subordinate halls or lodges. These are three, as they are arranged, the Egyptian being first on account of its antiquity, and on either side are the Norman and Ionic. The Egyptian hall is 65 feet long and 50 wide, and 30 feet high, and is the only perfect specimen of Egyptian architecture in America. It looks an extraordinary room on account of the massive and peculiar style of the Egyptian period. The furniture of this apart-

MASONIC TEMPLE AT PHILADELPHIA 109

ment is also characteristic. The Master's throne and
chair are weighty and imposing, and are gilded whereon
His pedestal, standing at his right hand, is flanked
by two mysterious sphynxes who gaze upon the
beholder, and the chair is flanked by two eagles.
The pedestals of the Senior and Junior Wardens are
all uniquely decorated, and the sofas provided have
capacity to seat about 200 brethren at once. The
furniture throughout is solidly cherry covered with
black and gold reps, and the carpet is blue with an
admixture of other colors. This apartment being so
unlike any to be seen in America will always be
an object of curiosity to strangers and the entire
world. South of the Egyptian is the Ionic hall,
which is another subordinate lodge-room. This is
somewhat larger than the hall before described.
This hall is 75 feet long by 50 wide and 30 feet
high, and the decorations and the furniture are of the
purest Grecian Ionic type, elegant and graceful, but
not elaborate. The impression is one of a profound
or lasting character as in the former, the columns
are not so elaborate, but the architecture must
have many admirers. The hall is capable of being
lighted by skylight by windows on two sides, and
has ample ventilation no dust amount and at night
it is lighted up with handsome and powerful pendants.
The furniture is made of walnut, with redar and
butternut inlay, and covered with reps of blue and

gold. On the north-east corner of the building, and of the same dimensions as the Ionic, is another lodge-room, the Norman, and the apartment is a thorough example of Norman decorative art, and with its full furnishings is as perfect an example or representation of the order as can possibly be. The settees have luxuriant spring seats, which are covered with yellow leather, and the stations of the three officers are much admired. The furniture is made of walnut and fir, and in the carpet the dominant colour is blue.

There is a fourth subordinate lodge, which is on the main floor. It is called the Oriental Hall, is immediately below the Norman Hall, and is about the same size as the apartment above. This hall is in style throughout a brilliant example of Moorish architecture, and the Eastern character is carried out in the minutest details on walls, ceiling, cornices, woodwork, and furniture. The hall itself is one of the finest in the temple, all being in strict accord with Moorish style, having all the Saracenic brilliancy of colour and peculiarities of that showy style. The seats are covered with blue leather.

The principal floor is chiefly taken up with the two chief apartments of the building, the Grand Lodge Hall and the Grand Chapter Hall; one on the northern end, the other on the southern side, and a number of vestibules and waiting rooms; the remainder

are the Egyptian, Ionic, and Norman Halls. The
Grand Lodge and Grand Chapter Halls are elevated
to the roof of the temple, so that the upper floor of
all only extends over a portion of the principal floor.
On the upper floor is the Asylum of the Commandery,
the only purely Gothic hall in the building, with its
attendant Council Chambers, waiting rooms, armory,
and separate apartments for each respective commandery. The building altogether contains one Grand
and six Subordinate Lodge Rooms, one Grand and
two Subordinate Chapter Rooms; an Asylum Council
Chamber, and attendant apartments for the Knights
Templar, a Library, and a multitude of small apartments.

The hall of the Grand Lodge is the representative
apartment of the temple, and the largest one in it. It is
105 feet long, 50 wide, and 50 high. There is an
octagonal vestibule at one end and you enter through
massive doors, which are artistically constructed of
walnut, and the panels are raised on moldings of cedar
wood; the panels are molded walnut and highly
polished. The furniture of this hall is walnut and
cedar, covered with blue plush, and the seats arranged
round the hall will accommodate about 400. There
are large gaseliers to light the hall at night, and the
glass in the roof is so constructed that sufficient light
is admitted during the day to light the hall. The
hall throughout is of the Corinthian order, everything

being in consonance with that style, and this like the other is intended as studies, as well as being representative, in both aggregate and detail, as perfect examples. The Corinthian Hall is replete with Masonic emblems. Conspicuous and central on the north and south façades are ornaments representing the working tools of the Freemason, and figures emblematic of architecture. On the corners are fragments of an Egyptian capital, to which the figures holding the tools are pointing. The east and west façades contain ornaments representing the corn, the wine, and the oil; in the centre of the east end are the platform and station of the Grand Master, and over it are the square and compass and rising sun. In the south is the Junior Grand Warden, and over it the sun at high noon. In the west is the Senior Grand Warden's station, and the emblem of the closing day marks his position. The magnificence of this apartment is enhanced by its great size and height, and the elaborate ornamentation and the appropriateness of the entire furnishings and adjuncts are completed in like grand and appropriate style. Before quitting this centre of Masonic interest, we have to say, as we feel, the grandeur of this temple inspires and impresses the visitor the moment he enters. Above is the broad artificial skylight, curiously intersected and wrought, tending to modify the light. On the left are four large windows, surmounted by a single cornice, and divided by Corinthian columns. On the right hand similar columns enclose the Warden's chair, and in the distance the Grand Master's chair, of walnut and cedar, is set in a recess with a canopy. All around are the cornices surmounted with a series of cones reaching to the skylight above, rich with festoons of flowers and leaves ornamenting the columns.

The brilliant lights from the sparkling gasoliers falling on the rich plush blue, and the varied colored carpet; the pedestal, created with the same material as it, stands in the centre of the lodge, with open Bible laid out beneath the flood of light falling from the great lights above, the fullness the vastness and completeness of the place, makes it a luminous and impressive exponent of the laws and the government of the order, and of the exceptional and solitary position this one holds in relation to the other lodge-rooms in the world.

The apartment designed as the meeting-place of the Grand Chapter is a companion to the above in magnificence, though it is a degree smaller. It is still a very large room, differing only from the other in length. It is 90 feet by 50 feet and 50 feet in height, the decorations and furnishing are in the Italian Renaissance style of architecture. Throughout the walls and ceilings are seen the emblems peculiar to Royal Arch Masonry displayed in their peculiar form. The skylights, constructed like the other, shed a profusion of modified light by day, and at night the hall is illuminated by a series of elaborately-finished gasaliers. In the centre of the eastern end of the hall is the triple chair of the high priest, king, and scribe peculiar to this degree of Masonry. In this, like the other apartments, the whole furniture is of the richest character, being made of walnut and inlaid with mahogany and Californian redwood. Red is the prevailing colour here, as blue is in the Grand and other lodge halls. A striking feature of this apartment is the veils of the temple, which are subordinate in the performance of some of the mysteries of of Royal Arch Masonry. Four high and beautiful arches are sprung across the room midway between the floor and ceiling; from each of these depends a veil. These veils contain twelve hundred yards of the best French satin; a nicely-adjusted windlass raises them, and is done in a few seconds when necessary. The room throughout is entirely emblematic of the various degrees of the Chapter, and is in every way as magnificent as the Grand Lodge Hall. It is entered from a vestibule of exquisitely-finished woodwork, and surrounded with the adjacent apartments necessary for the work, convenience, and comfort of the Companions in conferring the degrees. In the vestibule is a fountain of variegated marble, 12 feet high, and the whole furniture of it and waiting room are matched to correspond to the furnishing of them both in elegance of finish and appropriateness of design. The brilliant colours in the Grand Chapter Hall are dazzling to a degree. Crimson is the prevailing colour of the carpet and furniture, whilst the walls are white, crimson, purple, and blue. The rainbow-hued complexion or arrangement of colouring operated on by the radiance of the light from above almost deprives the architecture of its proper and natural effect. An elaborate porch surmounts the throne and triple chair and an organ of very fine construction fills a recess in the northern wall. The effect of this apartment on the visitor is entirely of a different kind to that experienced in the Grand Lodge Hall. Both are impressive, both thorough representations of the Masonry to be taught within them; but the rich brilliancy of colour in the Chapter Hall will always be the prevailing remembrance of its character and beauties.

Before I refer to any of the apartments which are chiefly accessory and subordinate, I will refer to those which are of a higher degree and which are devoted to the gallant and curious brethren of the craft, the Knight Templars. Their room is known as the asylum, and it has an adjacent Council Chamber, a drill room and banquet hall, and a smaller room intended for regalia, and probably room for the five Commanderies, and the other auxiliary apartments necessary for the service of the renowned Order. The asylum is 90 feet by 45 feet, and 40 feet high, and extends across the building from north to south. This is the only Gothic apartment in the whole building. There are displayed the cross and crowns, the emblem of the knights, and they appear in all the decorations. The gasaliers are a compound of crowns and crosses wrought together with artistic skill, but the Gothic feature is never lost in the complex intermixture. The same style is evinced in the furniture and its decoration, and is covered with green leather. Two lines of seats extend round the asylum. A lofty platform bears the richly-ornamented seats of the principal officers, the Commander, Generalissimo, Captain General, and Prelate, and behind these is the organ. In the Red Cross degree, the first of the Knightly orders, a necessary adjunct is the Council Chamber. This apartment is west of the chief one, or the Asylum, and is 40 by 25 feet wide and 25 feet high, and has all the necessary facilities for the pilgrim warrior. An ample avenue extends entirely around the Asylum, and in it are placed three tents for the guards. In connection with this degree there is a banquet hall, which is 75 feet long and 35 feet wide, and 20 feet high. This hall will seat 250 persons, and has all the culinary attachments necessary. Like the other apartments, this one is decorated with all the emblematic lore of this degree, and each Tem-

plar has a closet for the keeping of his arms, uniform,
and craft decorations.

Besides the banquet hall referred to, there is
another which is on the first floor, and this hall,
which the brethren intend for the great feasts which
are a part of the fraternal whole, occupies the greatest
part of one side of the main floor, and is 105 feet
long by 50 wide, and 30 feet high. Its architecture
is the Composite order. A double row of sixteen
columns divide it, their capitals being decorated with
birds, fruits and flowers. The turkey, the chief of
gastronomic fowls, presides over the main entrance,
and is magnificently suggestive of the rites which
receive the attention and are disposed of by the
brethren in this apartment of the Temple. The room
is capable of seating 500 persons at once. There are
twenty tables which can be made to suit the extent
of the company. There are fifteen gasaliers to light
up with a copious stream of light the whole apartment, and in a conspicuous position there is a statue
of Temperance to remind the jubilants of the extent
of their "table law." The floor is made of hard
wood and is tile covered. There is an apartment
which is closely allied to this one, and it is necessary
to refer to it, which is equal to any to be found in
any hotel in the country. It has a monster range and
all the other means for securing good cooking and
preparing palatable dishes for their festivities on such

feast days. I have not referred to this part of the house in the manner of giving it any prominence, but simply because it is an incidental concomitant to the festal displays which are associated with the Order, for the Library would fall naturally to be noticed, on account of its being the source of sustenance to the nobler part of the members. It is situated in one corner of the main floor, and its architecture is Italian Rennaissance, and is 65 feet long and 45 feet wide, and 30 feet in height, and is amply lighted on the two outside walls; nine rows of columns divide it, and they are placed in pairs, and it is fitted up with walnut bookcases in the centre of the room, whilst there are newspaper stands, reading tables, and other articles of library furniture, and the whole are intended for use as well as ornament, and to form a complete Masonic library for culture and general reference by the brethren.

It will be observed that each hall in the Temple is a sample of a different order of architecture, Freemasonry itself being the patron of architectural art, and in the Masonic edifices it should be the chief aim to give expression to this fact. This Temple in design has been made to give a model in completeness and a material and substantive embodiment of this idea to the world. We have in the various apartments the Egyptian, the Corinthian, the Doric, Ionic, Oriental, Norman and Gothic, the Italian Ren-

naissance, and the composite orders of architecture,
each being a complete study of its special subject. The
walls, ceiling, furniture, carpets and other fixtures are
made consonantly with these orders. The carpets
were made in Great Britain from designs furnished
by the Architect, so that they thoroughly harmonize
with the fittings and furnishings.

There is only one other lot of apartments that I
have to refer to. These are those belonging to the
grand officers, and are on the main floor. The Grand
Master is head of the whole Order in Pennsylvania,
and is elected annually, but generally holds office for
two years, being head of the craft and representative
of King Solomon. His apartments are prepared and
completed in a manner and style commensurate with
his official dignity and importance. There are three
rooms opening the one into the other. The first is
the reception, the next the Grand Master's, and the
third a private secretary's bureau, and a toilet room
is connected to the whole. The decorations are rich
and elaborately Masonic. The covering of the furniture is blue leather. Ingrained on the polished walnut of one of the main doors is a curious Masonic
delineation of the compasses, square, and all-seeing
eye which seemingly without any design appears in
the wood work and is calculated to attract considerate
and marked attention on account of its being a new
application of decorative art on wood that is real and

not imitated, and therefore regarded as consonant with the other strange symbolism of this ancient and mysterious fraternity. The Grand Secretary and Grand Treasurer have rooms close by, and they are richly furnished, and every suitable convenience is provided for themselves and their assistants.

As I stated before, the cost of the Temple and ground on which it stands was the large sum of 1,475,000 dols., and that money has been raised by virtue of a Masonic loan, on the powers of an Act of the Legislature of Pennsylvania, passed at the time operations were commenced, authorising the Grand Lodge to borrow money at not more than eight per cent., and the loan is the investment of all the lodge funds, and other Masonic bodies and Masonic charity funds are about one half, and the balance they have from various other sources. The old Temple, which stands in one of the best business streets in the city, must, when sold, yield to them a considerable amount of the balance, as I noticed it was in the market at the time the new one was consecrated in September last, when one of those pageants was witnessed which only Masons can accomplish, and which for grandeur was never equalled in this city of Philadelphia.

CHAPTER X.

PHILADELPHIA.

My stay in Philadelphia was prolonged beyond what I had at first intended, as at this point I expected letters from home, and I waited until I received them, however. I do not think it was on account of my protracted stay that I made the acquaintance of a little creature with a Spanish name, which is very importunate, in the evenings especially, to fascinate you with a peculiar musical lullaby about the time of retiring to bed. Up to this time I was not aware of having had the smallest mark of attention bestowed upon me by this delicate being. I had seen in some of the windows as I passed along a thin fabric or transparent covering for protection as against the onslaught of this sanguinary courtier, but I never for a moment considered that it was necessary to shield myself against the enticing importunities of any creature at bed-time, and resolved to pay no attention to a practice which I supposed was only carried out by the most officious, and as I had so fortunately eluded and escaped up to this time, I inferred that I would be safe for the future. I don't know that these creatures have any means of arriving at a knowledge of any resolution a person may take, or that they can be actuated by any feelings akin to revenge, for if I thought of any course of action in regard to them, certainly I never expressed it to any one; but on going home one night I fancied my concert was likely to be over musical, if not discordant. The attendance I thought was unreasonably large, and I began to consider what was best to be done. Before this time I had seen on the walls of my bedroom marks which up to this night had escaped my notice as to their real character, but now these marks were impressively suggestive as to their real existence; and as pictures often suggest to the mind first thoughts and then action, which at other times are foreign to it, so now I looked on these spots in the same light as Macbeth looked on the vision of the instrument he was about to use, and I resolved to clear the room, and having made a formal declaration of war, it was my intention it should be a *combat a l'outrance*, and having as I thought fully decimated the ranks of these winged syrens, I extinguished the "flaming minister," and consigned myself to the pleasures of dreamland. It is scarcely necessary for me to say that I awoke in the morning, and it was a favourable circumstance that I had resolved to leave the city for other scenes, for those who had made my brief acquaintance would have failed to identify me, or they might have asserted, as is sometimes done, in a manner so that they had wakened the strong powers." I may say it is quite possible for a person from this country to undergo a complete and thorough transformation in one night by means of the vindictive and adventurous addresses and caresses of that race which inspires the Yankee with more fear than the bigoted opposition of the prairies, and the wisest thing for a person to do who goes from this country to visit the States is to take as much mentality, prepared and ready as will envelope his head and hands so that he may be defended against the attacks of mosquitoes. It is indeed a small matter but to arrive at a full understanding of the extent to which it operates on and influences many of the social aspects of Yankee character would require a long stay on that continent, or to listen to the endless stories of the experience of those who have suffered ordinary or who have been eye-witnesses of the sufferings and similar ones of others. These speeches are delivered and embellished with energy for many and all the fervour inspired by lesser achievements so much so as to make you feel you were listening to some martial incidents of the "utmost deadly import," and you will hear reference to these occurrences in the alley the orchestra the forum the platform the pulpit the press the workshop the road the rail the river and especially the basement or the stoves to

this side the Atlantic. When anybody has nothing to say, the encounters and escapades with the mosquitoes immediately serve to fill up the gap, and everybody is at home at once, for everyone has one thing or another to say about them; and every *savan* you encounter, especially if he sees that their arrows have been levelled at you with poisoned effect, is ready to give you his advice *gratis* as to what you should do to ward off their future attacks, or to enable you to get quit of your present disfiguration; but it is all to no purpose, and they only waste their eloquence and your money, if you are foolish enough to follow their advice; for, despite the overwhelming array of talent and the numerical strength of the enemy, and the scientific appliances for the destruction of this insect, Miss Mosquito remains in possession of her position and is likely to do so.

The inventive brain of the American has been active to find some means to destroy this insect, and many compounds are offered for this purpose, and those which are the most effective are of that character whereof it is difficult to say of the bane or the antidote which is best or worse; and to any person who is desirous to make his fortune in the States, if he would set his ingenuity to work and discover some compound which would rid the natives only of these troublesome attendants, he would eclipse the name and fame of George Washington, as a conquerer and benefactor of a higher type, and his benefaction would receive the highest acclaim of the people and his labours would be accepted as inaugural of the great centennial pageant which will be consummated in this city in 1876. Everything in the States is magnified into a wonder or of a gigantic character, and when this is the case we can afford to admit it. Even the little world, or the insect world, is a great world of itself, and I think on this point like many other Americans must beat all creation. I am not going to submit an entomological dissertation, but I will refer to one or two insects which must have attracted the attention of every one who is desirous of being considered an observer of nature in this part of the empire. The tobacco worm and the walnut worm are the two largest, and are very striking as worms, and as flies they resemble one another in various particulars. As a grub they are about four inches long, and the prevailing colour is a clear pale green, with stripes of a deep gold colour, and ribbed with black. On the head of the walnut worm are six or eight large horns which give it rather a formidable appearance, to a certain extent not unlike a lobster, and in this state it passes the first year of its existence, and in the following year your attention is more directly attracted to it, for it appears to fly along near to bushes quite like a bird, and again its colours are showy, and it is no longer

antennæ, which are about six inches in length, whereby it sucks the nectar from the flowers, but its food are the leaves of the tomato, potato, or the tobacco plant. The minor insects are numerous beyond computation. One evening, while driving out in an open carriage, and passing under the branches of a tree which hung down very low, so that they were disturbed, there came such a shower of moths of all sorts that I felt inclined to jump out and leave them in possession; and the air was crowded here and there with shoals of them, enjoying the beams of the setting sun; but these are a poor substitute for the warblers which we have at home, and which at night make the woods vocal with their melody, besides preventing the undesirable growth of those insects which infest all vegetable life. The few birds which they have are only short-stayed in any part of the country, and are continually on the wing; and it will be a long time before the sparrow will propagate sufficiently to overtake all the work that is wanted to be done on the Continent of America.

I have been induced to make these remarks about insect life on account of my interest in the mosquito. There is no fear of any one forgetting them who has had the close intercourse with them that I have had. It sometimes makes all the difference that can be in a traveller's experience the kind of position of the room he has allotted to him at an hotel. Strangers

don't know this, and in the busy season they are not
particular to inform strangers to look out for these
disturbers of the peace. By the way, I don't remember
having seen any domestic pets in America. Dogs,
cats, and parrots are to be found in abundance at
home, and any number of birds, but I can't remember a solitary instance where I saw the one or the
other during my stay there. Yes; there was one instance, only one that I can remember and it was
the only one and such a one I should not have forgotten. It was a dog, and its colour was a clear and
decided magenta, and I was disposed to think that it
was originally a white dog and had been dyed, and
as the ear that I was in passed, it ran out from a shop
barking, and I concluded it was used as a sort of advertising medium; but it was certainly startling in
its appearance on account of its colour, and its owner,
I have no doubt, thought it was a clever trick. The
lady is the great domestic pet in the States, as it is
here, but as they are very difficult to rear there it
has a decided influence on their character, and whilst
they are very young they talk like a book, and they
are regarded as prodigies which can only be produced in that part of the world. Babies and parrots
are equally clever and the wives are as sparkling and
'cute as the husbands, and to do anything utterly
promiscuous on behalf of the husband should follow
would be out of the question, and on that account

domestic felicity is rare and divorce is cheap and exceedingly common; and many take the advantage of the legal facilities to begin life anew, not always to give manifestation of having improved by the change. Marriages are consummated at a very early age, and it is not considered necessary to have a house of one's own. Lodgings are always easily procured, and housekeeping is the exception, not the rule. Working men are more migratory in their habits, and the distance they have often to remove is much greater than at home here, and this has an effect in sending them into lodgings rather than housekeeping. The genuine American working-man is a person of a different type and character from what we have at home, and what is true of him is true of every one who labours in America. They all work hard, and the senseless and extreme short-time movement seems to get little or no countenance amongst them. Whether this is the effect of decided love of labour, or of a superior knowledge of political economy to what is evinced by labourers at home I don't know, but they seem to understand that by curtailing working hours and doing nothing during that curtailed working time would so enhance their labour that the chances were to throw it out of the market and shift their labour to some other field where it could be more cheaply done, hence they produce more for the same amount of money than is done at home here,

and if they want to increase their incomes they work
harder or they work more time, and they thereby
show they understand the only solid basis on which
to better their condition so far as labour is concerned.
And what is true of them as labourers is true of them
as citizens; the general type of the labourer has been
moulded very much by the character of the men who
have at various times emigrated from other countries
to the States, these being usually of a better class
to those left in the mother countries, and the effects of
this is obvious in their general character and deportment. The working-man is a gentleman when off
duty, his general attire bespeaks it so far as his
attire can do so, and those who wish it syllabled in
stronger terms or language are wont to do so by
means of the incontrovertible evidence of jewel-
lery. I saw one elaborate specimen in Brooklyn,
who perhaps might pass muster in that part of
the world, but for my part I could not see it. He
might have been a very good tradesman or mechanic,
but I considered him a very bad hand at personal
decoration. However, if they do not at all times succeed in attiring themselves tastefully, they are almost
always sure to be cleanly, and so far as I could see
one might go the round of the States and not see so
much filth, squalor, rags, and misery, nor feel such
vile and offensive odours, as are to be seen and felt
in our passage along our streets. There may be

physical advantages or disadvantages on this or that side. There may be moral or social advantages or disadvantages on this or that side. I merely state the facts as I found them, and as I have heard done so by others who have been on both sides. If there is anything which is a source of pleasure or gratification to one on visiting the other side, it must be the general cleanliness of the people, which never fails to attract attention everywhere, and at all times it is noticeable, and strangers are always sure to observe it; and if it is the case at the time or season when strangers go abroad, we may naturally presume such is the case at other times of the year as well. Another feature one cannot fail to observe is the prevalent practice of early rising. I am not disposed in the least to attribute this to the universal adoption of the maxims of their great philosopher Franklin. I rather think it is caused by a greater amount of vitality in the air than is possessed in Britain. It is said it is to get through business before the heat gets too oppressive. Of course the shadows are deeper and longer in the morning, but the heat of the sun, according to my calculation, was as great at its first appearance as at any time of the day. I was disposed at times to think my watch had become sluggish, the folks were so much in advance of our home customs. Between eight and nine in the morning great numbers of ladies were abroad for all purposes, not a rush out in some *dishabille* but fully attired for the day. Of course breakfasting is past at an early hour and dinner takes place at midday, but there, as here, the number who dine at home is limited, and especially so in hot weather. I was very much struck by seeing the streets of Philadelphia more than usually crowded by ladies on a Saturday afternoon, and being curious to discover the kind of attraction which drew them all in a particular direction, I was induced to follow the stream, and found them pouring into a building built of white marble, and from various characteristic emblems I saw on the front elevation I was sure it was a theatre, and a matinee performance was about to be given for those who could not make it convenient to attend in the cool of the evening, and I thought, like "Peeping Tom," if the character of the entertainment was suitable for ladies, it might be so for gentlemen also, and I thought I might now get a glance of seeing a corresponding feature of American life elsewhere, so I determined to take the advantage of this opportunity. I did not learn whether this was the last or the most fashionable house of the kind in the city, but the quality of the dresses indicated that they were well up in the social scale, and I presume the house would be regarded as suitable to the folks that filled its benches. I tried to secure a seat, but that was beyond the limits of the house, at least that part where I was, and the ladies had possession of all the available space. However, as my business was chiefly to take notes, I was as well pleased, for it enabled me to look about. The assembly was quite a rare one. I had never seen such an imposing and attractive gathering. Here and there I could see a solitary gentleman, for in many instances where one was he was so thoroughly covered up with the light and airy habiliments of the fair sex that he was with difficulty seen at all, and this state of things rather interfered with me in getting anything like an accurate estimate of the proportion of the audience composed of gentlemen; and after an effort or two I concluded there would be about five per cent., and they were all reckoned as belonging to good society. I had ascertained this before going in, and I made sure that the quality of the entertainment would be of the same kind, but I was somewhat startled to find it a sort of adaptation of "Jack Sheppard," with the names of the characters and the incidents slightly altered, and the whole merit of the piece lay in the voluble speeches and the sprightly acting of a young lady who played the part of the hero of the piece, and the scenes were all laid in the British metropolis.

On a former occasion I alluded to the dead heroes of the late rebellion. They are out of sight of course, but their memory is preserved in the way I mentioned before by planting the national flag over their

graves every year on "Decoration Day." But there
is one other class of heroes next in the list as regards
honour, for they carry the silent but unequivocal
token of their actions in the field of battle, and do
not require to tell you they were there. I mean the
cripple, and these, like the poor they will always have
with them for many years to come. Spoiled for the
labour they pursued before the war, they can only
follow that form of labour that can be made to fit their
condition, as that cannot be fitted to every kind of
labour. Great numbers are employed about the
Government offices in the capital and similar positions in the larger cities.

This city has been selected for the grand display
which will take place in 1876, the Centennial Celebration of Independence. Possibly the suitableness of
the country around the city has induced the commis-
sion to decide on Philadelphia as the place for it, the
country and facilities in and around being quite suited
for such an exposition or pageant as will take place
on that occasion. Hotel keepers are turning their
attention to the prospective and certain requirements
of the myriads who will wend their way to witness
this wonderful and startling event. All former
efforts of Britain, France, and Germany are to be for
ever and effectively eclipsed. A structure commensurate with the size and character of the claims of
the continent and people will be built, the whole

force and array of inventive genius and national talents will be convoked; the productions of other countries will be accepted, but only to show the surpassing and significant advance made by the New World on the creations of the inventive art of the Old. The attractions are to draw by their superior influence the Laplander, the New Zealander, the Japanese, the Russian, and invest them with the genuine spirit of enterprise and progress. And the high and accepted representative embodiments of learning, culture, and refinement from the polished and advanced portions of the world; to show them how dim, obscure, crude, and undefined all their previous study and labours have been, compared with the dazzling array of art treasures which will occupy this new and stupendous Temple of Art, which will in three years hence adorn the ample and level grounds in the suburbs of Philadelphia.

CHAPTER XI

EN ROUTE FOR NIAGARA.

As the winged insect, which has revelled amidst a profusion of gay and luxuriant flowers, turns its back upon them after having extracted from their fulness a load of honeyed wealth, so does the traveller on the scenes which were at first invested with interest and full with all the freshness of novelty and attraction, leaving them to others who will come and find them as fragrant, pleasing and inspiring as if they had never afforded the same enjoyment to those who preceded them. When once in the States the traveller is never at a loss to find scenes both very startling and attractive, but the question interposes itself, whether these scenes are equal to the reports one hears of them in Britain, and the only means one has of ascertaining the fact and dispelling the labor of curiosity which shrouds him is to go and get the ocular proof and satisfy himself. This is by no means easily done, on account of the magnitude of the country, but no labour is grudged when once you are thoroughly imbued with the curiosity I have referred to. The most wonderful sight so far as report goes are those celebrated Falls, which are no the confines of the United States, and divide them from British North America, along with the chain of lakes and rivers connected with them. And one almost instinctively turns in that direction, expecting to find what will repay him for his trouble and expense. The road from Philadelphia to Niagara is rather a long one, being nearly equal to a run from Land's-end to John o'Groats; but as there is much of interest by the road to one who has travelled it for the first time, he does not feel it to be an undertaking of such a formidable character, and as the route of the railway by this line is considered to be rather attractive, the journey is rather a pleasant one. Of course one cannot make the whole run during the day, but what one sees from morning to night is strikingly different from what is to be seen on any other line in this country. If one could always manage to pursue his journey by daylight his pleasure and store of knowledge would be considerably enhanced, but that is not always possible where there is much to do and little time to do it in. If there are other routes as interesting as the one by which I went, I can only console myself by the reflection that I could only travel by one at a time, and that it was the best to my liking. The train, on leaving Philadelphia, proceeds by the Lehigh, the Susquehanna, and the Wyoming Valleys, affording a relishable admixture of the various phases of nature in her

primeval beauty and wildness, the grandeur and
eloquence of her visible attributes and the external
bulky and material evidences of her beauty in the
treasures which we see as we proceed on through the
district of Pennsylvania, for we are not long on our
travels till we meet trains of waggons of great length
with coal, iron, lime, cement, and petroleum, and
there are thousands of hands extracting these rough
and rugged materials from the mountain and the
mine, and by the alchemy of labour transmuting
them into the golden treasure, the reward of industry.

In a run of so many miles there must of course be
a very great number of places, but it is only a limited
number which is worthy of being noticed. A small
village composed of wooden huts on a comparatively
level district is not of sufficient interest to attract
one, especially when every minute you expect to see
some imposing sight which is calculated to take
away your breath and sink everything else into the
obscurity of neglect. The first place which is calculated to claim a passing thought from one is the town
of Bethlehem. It is not of any extent but is scattered, and has all the rough and unimproved appearance of a place which has been hurriedly called into
existence, and will be set to rights when once the inhabitants will get time to do so. But everywhere
there is a press of business, and great activity is
observable. The canals are crowded with timber,

and running over with the full stream which is continually rushing through the Lehigh Valley. Gigantic piles of wood—or lumber as they call it—are crowding all the available spaces, and look like so many huts. The houses are chiefly of wood, the plaster on the inside walls being the only incombustible material about them. Numerous mills and workshops are to be seen, and numbers of commercial men are leaving the train to prosecute their callings; and there are those who are in quest of the change the highlands afford, for the train keeps going uphill during its whole course—not hurriedly, but still going up. The course is uniformly along the margin of the stream, and many curiously wild and romantic scenes are passed. The river at some of the mountain gorges is narrow, and rocks, trees, and remnants of the ravages of storms are lying wedged and huddled together in an inextricable heap, but at the same time truly picturesque. The mountains at some of the points rise to a considerable height, and are copiously wooded; and the canals are well filled with loose timber for cutting at the manufactories, or for sending down intact to the market. Trains of immense length are seen coming from the carbon country, running along the opposite bank of the river, on their way to the large cities. After we have run for a considerable time we arrive at a place which is of a striking character. It is ensconced in a beautiful

corner of creation, nestling amongst richly wooded
hills, and is only seen a second or two before the cars
dash into it by an acute curve in the line. It has
an Indian name not at all musical to British ears, but
we can overlook that if we are allowed to enjoy the
beauties which surround the capital of the carbon
country of Mauch Chunk, for the Americans call it
the Switzerland of America. The part of it which is
seen from the rail gives strong evidence of being
inhabited by enterprising and tasteful people. The
villas are chiefly composed of brick and in a conspicuous place is seen the residence of one of the carbon
kings, the Hon. Asa Packer, surrounded by finely
wooded enclosures, and tastefully arranged grounds,
floral devices and groups of statuary. There are
others of a similar description. The general surroundings and the country are singularly attractive,
but the chief of its attractions for the tourist is the
exciting ride over the Switchback. The railway runs
on its run up the hill to between 600 and 700 feet,
on a plane of over 2000 feet long, about one foot in
three, and then you stand on the top of Mount
Pisgah. It is said there is no cause for fear or
timidity in making the ascent, but for my own part
I had to hold go up with Professor Wyss. It is said
the sight from this height is the finest in America,
and the run along the highlands when once up, is
unsurpassed for variety of scenery no extent being

some eighteen miles, and all worked by stationary engines, which make the ride most steady and pleasant to the tourist. Very many frequent this attractive spot in the fine time of the year, and you can see villas spotting the hill sides, looking out from among the varied-coloured trees which surround them on all sides. Shortly after leaving this station a person from one of the hotels at a station some distance in the direction in which we are going joins the cars, with the view of ascertaining how many are likely to dine at the hotel, and at the next station he telegraphs forward, and when we arrive at Whitehaven we get 20 minutes for dinner, but no time to look about; but we cannot fail to notice that there is much stir and activity in every line connected with the timber and its branch trades. In some of these places, remote from large commercial centres, wood is cut and formed and adapted for building purposes, and has only to be fixed when it comes into the carpenter's hands; for nearly all the houses in the places which have grown up in the forests are built of wood, the only other material about them being the iron of the stove and pipes, and the plaster when the inner walls are furnished in that manner. When dinner is completed we start off again, and the next spot of note or interest is gained when we reach the summit of the hill or mountain which overlooks the valley of fair Wyoming. One can scarcely take in the extent

of landscape which is spread before him at this point,
neither would it be possible to see it were it not for
the facilities afforded by the position of the railway.
We have climbed up on our course several hundred
feet, and the train passes just at the upper end of the
valley; and as it takes some time to pass this point,
one has ample time to see the whole wide-spread panorama before him. The interest too, is enhanced at
this point by the character of the country through
which the cars pass. For some time before we
come to the spot at which we can see this magnificent scenery, the train runs through a wood of considerable depth, and now and again a glimpse of the
interminable and undulating forests is got on one
side, with scarcely a break or opening as far as the
eye can grasp the space. Hills rise over hills clad
in thick and solid array of leafy scenery only here
and there a thin pale streak of smoke, indicating the
abode of some squatter, new settler, or the bustle
marking the quiet and repose the busy city denizen;
and all at once, when one thinks he is lost in a sea
of forests, the amphitheatre of unsurpassed magnificence is seen to open up, bristling with beauty and
interest. On the hill-sides are seen the rich verdant
sylvan retreats, with their silver streams rippling and
winding on their courses to join the central river,
which is seen to widen as it pursues its tortuous
course in the direction of the sea. The distance seen

from this point must be over twenty miles down the valley, and about four or five across; and every spot looked to be carefully cultured. Towns and villages could be noticed on either side of the stream, which flows through the centre and the farm steadings, in the midst of compact and cultivated fields. Flocks and herds were browsing and reposing beneath the shadows of wide-spreading trees. Cottages were fretted and garnished with trails of Indian roses, like Gertrude's of old; and the spires of the village churches could be seen peering up through some consecrated spots. Nearly all the land rising towards the hill top is clothed with a profusion of groves, and the whole land, so far as one can see and judge, must have undergone careful cultivation, and for a longer period than any land that is seen for miles around. Looking at this place one can understand how reluctant the Indian would be to allow the paleface to take possession of this lovely spot, and the reason for the deadly strife which was waged between them for a long period before it was relinquished. As we pass along, the train seems to take to a certain extent the circle of the top of the valley, and there are openings in the woods and groves through which you can see the full extent of the valley from the various points or positions, making this sight one of the most varied, enchanting, and lovely which can be seen anywhere. A feeling steals over you as you leave this interest-

ing spot that you would like to roam over the fair
fields filled with a profusion of Nature's beauties, and
inhale the fresh odours from fragrant meadows, and
hear the soft cadence of the streams as they meander
through the rich and fertile slopes, or wander among
the ruins of the forts and defences and read their
past history, or the part they played in the scenes of
strife in its early history; but we are only permitted
to do so in fancy, as we are hurried past to view
other scenes which have not the soft drapery of culture to adorn them but the bold, broad and majestic
forms and beauties of primeval Nature. We have
passed the falls over which the stream finds its way
into the classic valley of Wyoming, and soar along
the banks of the Susquehanna which at some points
broadens into a sea and at others its waters rush
with impetuosity by some confined and narrow canon
until it finds some level bank when its silent cur-
rent is regained. For hundreds of miles we swerve,
jerky this-a-ways in its windings through the valley by
brook and bank, by stream and azure over brake and
gully. Villages and cities are passed and again
reveals, one with classic names, others resounding
one of those who are now driven into the remoter
part of this great continent, awaiting the forcing to-
curious of the race of men and to them, the terrible
smoking of the iron horse with its veins and ghostly
riders. On we sped as we pass the vale of Avon, and

Montrose on the other; Rome lies hidden by intervening hills and wood, and as the shades of night are about to clothe all nature in her sober livery, we reach the city of Athens, and we instinctively look about for any feature which was likely to form an ingredient in what induced those who named this place after the capital of Greece to do so; but we fail to discover any one of any kind in common with those gleaned from historic sources. On an extended plain, neither flanked nor backed with those gigantic forms of nature which inspire man to heroic deeds and aspirations for glory and immortal fame, it lies partially concealed. By the mean range of buildings in the main street there are no indications that any of the citizens have risen to opulence and ease. There are no *chateaux* on the confines of the place, no picturesque villas with dressed and cultured grounds and shady retreats, no well trimmed and regular fenced desmesnes; but the same features prevail which are common to all the newly formed places, where all these external trapping, adornments, and decorations are left till the more important and necessary works are efficiently done, and there is a raw and universal look of discomfort about the suburbs of these new places. The sun is set, and all the interest which daylight provides for the tourist is also set. There is no twilight, and the sober evening melts into darkness before you have time to see

any object under its influence. The lamps are
lighted, and the cars thunder along in the dark.
Numerous small villages are passed, and Elmira is
reached; another long run, and we come to Buffalo,
on the confines of Lake Erie; and after changing we
have a brief run along the banks of the Niagara
River for a few miles, and the Falls are reached after
a drive of about 18 hours. The night is clear,
the stars are bright and sparkling, and the moon is
beginning to throw a melancholy light over the surrounding gloom. Though it is one o'clock in the
morning there are six or seven 'busses waiting to
convey the passengers to the hotels they represent,
and the characteristic energy and volubility of their
drivers are profusely used to convince you how close
this or that hotel is to the Falls, but as there is
always some one at hand to keep you right, and as
there is an impossibility of selecting more than one,
I selected that one and getting in, I arrived at a private hotel. After getting a glass of the best south-
side Madeira, I ascended to my chamber's number
with my brain filled with a confused and interminn-
able array of sights and objects I had seen on the
way to this upper storey of the American continent.
I opened my window to see if anything could be seen
of the mighty flood, but various objects barred the
way, and nothing could be seen but here and there a
solitary tree with its foliage gleaming in the silver

A

rays of the rising moon; but all the air was filled with a soft hissing sound coming from the restless, seething, foaming, boiling waters which were pouring over the Falls of Niagara.

CHAPTER XII

THE FALLS OF NIAGARA.

THE sun's rising had preceded mine by several hours, and when I got up and looked out of my window I found hill, house, and hamlet, lake, lawn, and landscape, gilded by his warmth and life-inspiring light. The air was light and elastic, and was filled with the same volume of sound which hushed all around to sleep the night before. But now all was life, bustle, and activity. To one who has dreamt of this great sight for half a lifetime, and who knows he is about to realise it, the sensation is strange beyond description. To be at the Falls with the knowledge of seeing them in a few seconds is like to take away your breath. You cannot help thinking what is common to all—this is the greatest sight in the world and now you have only to step aside and see it. You cannot forget your position in this respect, for were you to do for doing so, the sound, like the fascinating eye of the Cobra, would draw you to the spot. To approach them from the American side is impossible, for every available spot where the sight is worth a cent is utilized, and you are compelled to seek the bridge and pass to the Canadian side before you can see the world-famed cascade to advantage; and it is evidently the most natural spot for this on Table Rock. The whole picture lies before you, and every spot along the picture can be explored with the eye, and the sight is one which for grandeur and magnificence places it beyond the power of any one to describe; and many, under the consciousness of this feebleness of language to convey the idea of it to others, have been guilty of every absurdity in relation to height and other features connected with this great avalanche of water.

There is much in the way or manner you see a sight for the first time. Many are disappointed on looking at the Falls for the first time; and I think that arises from the fact that the water falls from the level on which the spectator stands down into a gully, glen, or canon, and the sides of the river rise up to your platform, almost perpenicular to that height, and on that account one feels disposed rather to lessen their magnitude than increase it. And on this principle one is astonished to hear of the exaggerated accounts from those who first saw and described them. The Jesuit father Hennepin called them 600 feet, Baron La Houten 700 or 800 feet, and Charlevoix 140 feet; but as in the earlier accounts the language is feeble and infantile, they tend, as I said before, to remedy the defect by increasing their magnitude. There are many points from which the

visitor can contemplate these wonderful torrents, but
to get a just conception of their magnitude and
power the bank of the stream below is certainly the
best; and this is advanced by those who are most
interested in the enterprise and no argument is
wanting to incline you to see the mysteries of this
marvel from the lower level. You admire the disinterestedness of these people and believing by the
descent you are likely to add materially to your
stock of knowledge, you allow yourself to be melted
into acquiescence, and you submit to the necessary
metamorphosis and leaving your outward crust in a
corner you sally forward habilitated, defying every
attempt at recognition by the nearest and dearest on
earth. There are few who have not seen some phase
of a seaman's life in a storm—the angry surges of the
flood and the sweeping showers of spray hurled
against him with force and frequency, requiring him
to be incased in his glossy sables to resist their fury
and defy their power. Suppose for a moment you
are such a figure as I have described moving forward
towards the bank of the Niagara on a fine sunshiny
day. Numerous pleasure parties are moving about,
cars and carriages are filled with gay and jubilant
crowds, and foot passengers are numerous by the
way you pass, but no one takes notice of you. Hundreds of oil-wearers and rustling oilskins have
passed that way before and the solitary dark figure

is allowed to pass and go down into the depths of the river and drown himself if he is disposed to do so. The descent is made by a spiral staircase, and you go down, down, and round, round, until you arrive at a bank of huge fragments of rock which have been detached from the mighty overhanging mass overhead. By this time you have forgotten all about the fine weather above, and you are now under the shadow of a great rock in a strange land. Fear comes upon you like an armed man, but you are comforted by the fellow at your elbow, who very likely tells you the rocks only come down in the winter time. You breathe a little freer, for it is some months to that time, and you hope to be four thousand miles off if you survive the present awful adventure; but still we are coming nearer the horrible watery abyss in front, and he opens his mouth to say something to you, and you are fain to put the words into his mouth, "Will you go back?" but no, "Take care of your feet." Heaven and earth! where is the fellow going? for he is now in front. Signs are substituted for words, for the thunder is raging over us, and the whirlwind is like to deprive us of the little breath remaining, and the spray is pelting and lashing over and around us. And now we stand behind a detached fall and look out on the scene before us. The whole is basking in light, and looks like sculptor work in white marble. The floods as they roll over and take their final leap into the seething and boiling cauldron below are white; the river as it rages and rushes through its confined channel is of milky whiteness, and we fancy everything is still without, and that the thunder and storm have followed us into the chasm before us. Our stay is brief, and we are thankful when we get the right-about-face. We clamber over the rocky bed, and take a philosophical and geological glimpse at the perpendicular wall on our left as we pass along; but we do not feel disposed to make our analysis a very elaborate or protracted one, lest our acquaintance be one of a striking character, and we hurry our investigation of the stratified calcareous materials, and are not particular to ascertain to what period they belonged. And after having tasted the sulphureous spring-water issuing from the rock, we deem it advisable to flee from where dangers are so rife, and where there are any immediate or remote chances of getting into the angry jaws of the flood below. We gain the foot of the ladder, and here we can safely, and with pleasure, cast our eyes about. It is only a new phase of the same, but every new point shows features attractive and grand, and this is a feature which is peculiar to the Falls. Place yourself on the hundred different points from whence a view is got, and you will find a special interest in them all. From this, right opposite to the American Fall, and it extends away to the left down in the direction in which the river Niagara flows for about a quarter of a mile; and the height is 164 feet, but the great breadth of it has the effect of lessening the height in appearance. At the lower end of it, a few yards apart, there is a small Fall, and it is called the Bridal Veil. It is a considerable sheet, and its fall is similar in height to the great Fall alongside. On the right of the American Fall is the Goat Island, and this island divides the two Falls. The island is about seventy acres in extent, and it is a very pleasant ramble by its shady lanes, among its birch, beech, oak, firs, and cedars. The portion of this island which intervenes between the Falls is small, and hence their continuity is little interfered with, making them appear as one. Then to the right the Canadian or Horse-Shoe Fall begins, and makes a circle of about half a mile, or double that of the the American Fall, and comes round to the point where we look from. But in looking at this great phenomenon from any solitary point, no just or accurate estimate of the quantity of water which falls from these rocks can be obtained; but if we were to trace the source whence the floods are derived, it might help us in the absence of facts arithmetically obtained. In the interior, and above this point, are six immense fresh-water lakes, and they are all united by rivers running from one into the other, thus forming a chain of lakes. There are Lakes Michigan, Superior, Huron, Erie, St. Clair and Simcoe. The latter two are small compared with the four former, some of which take several days to cross, being four or five hundred miles at some points, and from them the surplus water runs down the St. Lawrence, which virtually begins at the lower end of Lake Erie, running down the Niagara into Lake Ontario, and thence by way of Montreal and Quebec to the Atlantic Ocean. After having thus cursorily glanced at the sources from whence this flood is supplied, we can easily see the quantity to be very great, and some scientific men have attempted to reduce it to figures, and from the fact that some two or more have agreed in their results so far, we may accept it as a fair approximation to the truth. I will only give one short example, by a professor of an American college, who states the quantity which passes over these Falls in the minute to be fifteen hundred million of cubic feet, but this is only another proof of the feebleness of human language to express, or of the human mind to comprise, grasp or realise anything of that kind in relation to this wonderful work of nature. There is still another example, showing the magnitude of the mass of water which finds its way by this river to the ocean. On one occasion a vessel was chartered—we shall say—for this voyage, and the crew was composed of a four-

deer, buffalo, fox, and various other animals, and she was sent over the Falls. She drew 18 feet, and she passed over the Horse-Shoe Falls into the abyss below, proving the water on the shelf of the rock to be about 20 feet; and at that point the water is seen to be of a clear green colour, showing it to be an immense depth. The fall of such a body of water from such a height is sure to produce a variety of phenomena. At one time I noticed a column of spray just like a cloud, several hundred feet high, and the effect of the light of the sun by day and the moon by night on this body of vapour is curious, and grand at times; but this phenomena depends on the state of the atmosphere. Sometimes there is nothing worthy of notice there to characterise it from any other waterfall.

The river Niagara, from where it begins at the bottom of Lake Erie to the Falls, is about 22 miles, and from the Falls to Lake Ontario it is about 14, in all 36 miles. In that distance the Continent subsides between three and four hundred feet, the middle leap downward being over the Falls; and onward it rushes through the chasm, gully, or canon of 14 miles with stern and terrible velocity, tearing everything away which would dare check its progress to Lake Ontario. This gully along the whole passage is strikingly wild, romantic, and singularly grand, rising at a few points some 300 feet almost

straight up from the flood below, its stony shelves
profusely furnished with a variety of trees, shrubs,
and other vegetation, the varied colours of which are
fitly relieved by the grey, ribbed, and irregular stone-
work below. There are several places where rapids
are seen, but nothing like the rapid in this portion of
the river can be seen anywhere. There is one rapid
which is so grand in this river, some two miles or so
from the Falls, that the Yankee has utilised it and
made it private property, and tourists are entertained
to the sight at the charge of a shilling (25 cents) a
head. This is called the whirlpool rapids, and here
the water courses with such rapidity that you would
suppose there was a rock in the way, for the water
rises by its own force some 8 or 9 feet, making a
splash as it were sent up by a torpedo.

There is an amusing little episode connected with
this rapid. At one time a little steamer used to run
on the river between the American side and Canada.
She was called the Maid of the Mist, and her owner
getting into difficulties on account of a bond which
was over her, and legal proceedings threatened, he
determined to run the rapid, to stay proceedings by
getting into British water. Everybody thought such
an act impossible, as no vessel was ever known to
pass down the river, but the skipper resolved and
accomplished this terrible task with the loss of his
funnel only. His laurels were green ever after it,

and he is spoken of with much animation, and as much admiration for his courage.

This varied spot has induced much speculation in a geological point of interest, and no person can visit it without being struck with the character of the scenes. The upper river pursues its course through an open and ample plain, and at some parts is miles in breadth; but down at this rapid a person was known to throw a stone from one empire into the other, and nearly everywhere the sides rise from two to three hundred feet above the bed of the stream, marking it with a decidedly different character to that above the Falls. And it is thought that the river in its impetuous march and violent ebulitions has sapped and scoured the rocks from their beds, forming a deep chasm on the same level as the bed of Lake Ontario, and by doing so has called into existence the rich and romantic grandeur, and the endless phenomena which is everywhere seen in and around the Falls. Above the Falls the great rapids are the distinguishing feature. From the mouth of the Chippewa river the bed of the Niagara begins to slope towards the Falls, and the water receives a corresponding momentum, which increases until they make their final leap; and this declivity has been taken advantage of, and several mills and public works are set down by the side of the river for the water power. The fall, descent, or slope of the land in the distance

THE FALLS OF NIAGARA.   157

specified is some 50 feet, and by the time the waters
near the cataract their impetuosity is something
fearful. Boating is not safe within two miles, where
the smooth surface of the stream begins to ripple and
goes on increasing its impetus until it is lashed into
fury and roars like a sea in a hurricane. The breadth
of the stream immediately across the upper end of
Goat Island must be over a mile, and a considerable
bay is formed on the Canadian shore, round which
the water turns with a swoop, at times bearing down
all opposition. The mills referred to are on the
American side and have their connections with the
town of Niagara. Besides Goat Island there are
several small islands, called Bath, Luna, and the
Three Sisters. On Bath Island there is a paper mill
where the paper for the *New York Tribune* newspaper
is manufactured. All these islands are connected by
bridges from Niagara side, and are possessed by enterprising Yankees, who are bent upon extracting the
full value for the sights which are accessible by the
facilities afforded by them. I mentioned before that
every spot where a view can be obtained of the Falls
on the United States side is bolted, barred, and her-
metically sealed, except to the open sesame of cents
and dollars, but this is just carrying out a practice
which is experienced by all strangers in the States,
though it is here more seriously glaring on account
of the opposite practice pursued on the British side.

where one can roam from Lake Ontario to Lake Erie without hindrance, and enjoy all that is worthy being seen or enjoyed. On this side of the river is the village of Clifton, just by the Falls on the Canadian side as the town of Niagara is on the American bank, and the communication between is effected by means of the new suspension bridge, a modern and very graceful structure in iron, which spans the river at a spot twelve hundred feet across; from pier to pier it is nearly thirteen hundred feet, and is a hundred and ninety feet above the water surface, and well-nigh four hundred feet above the bed of the river, as its depth here is about one hundred and eighty feet. This bridge is exceedingly worthy of all that has been said about it. It is a fairy-looking piece of work—light, airy, and quite in keeping with the place and all its accessories; and one feature in connection with its construction is worthy of notice. The span is very great, and to relieve it from the pressure occasioned by storms or otherwise a great number of stays, of every degree of strength, are fixed between it and the banks of the river. These stays are forty-eight in number, and their weight fifteen tons. There are also a great number of guys, about or over fifty, giving the whole work a most intricate and unique appearance. The towers at the piers are one hundred feet high, and from the cables which support the bridge are some five hundred suspenders, giving the roadway the

appearance of a long and magnificent one. Light
carriages are allowed to pass over but not to halt on
the bridge. The change in temperature from winter's
cold to summer's heat produces a difference of three
feet in the height of the bridge by expansion and
contraction of the metal.

The old bridge is some distance further down the
river and much which has been said of the new one
is true of the old. The span is not so great, and
strength more than elegance was aimed at in its construction. It is used for a double purpose. Over it
the New York Central Railway forms a connection
with the Great Western, and there is a railway
underneath the railway. The cables are twice the
strength of those on the new bridge, and the towers
are about thirty feet less in height. The bridges are
of course in charge of persons who charge the traveller
who rides or passes on foot, and here also we have the
Custom-house officer of the "Bald Eagle." It seems
to matter little or nothing what you may buy in the
States and take across, no one challenges you by the
way. You are not subject to any State surveillance
on the British side; you can pass freely. But on
coming into the States the Custom-house officials must
know the amount of your purchases on the British
frontier, and have his fee ad valorem in the interest
of the "stars and stripes." The protection of the
rule of the United States seems to require a sleepless

and unremitting vigilance; for at any time, at every stage, on the frontier, the eye of the "eagle" must penetrate the inmost recesses of your baggage for the detection of contraband. To tourists it is an unsufferable nuisance, and at times you feel in a temper to be uncivil, and you are disposed to consider the treatment you undergo on the States territory as the result of a universal and well concerted conspiracy to treat every foreigner as a spy, undeserving either sympathy or the generous recognition which a stranger ought to receive on the part of those among whom he sojourns for a time. But as every one undergoes a successive process of fleecing before he gets this length, he does not expect an exceptional kind of treatment when he sojourns at the Falls of Niagara.

To a person whose proclivities or tendencies are of a scientific character much may be found at the Falls to interest him, for a person is very apt to ask, How is this? what is the cause of that? and, in the absence of a sufficiently qualified instructor, to aim at the solution of the difficulty at once, and on the spot. There are many natural phenomena which may be explained, and there are others which are certainly above explanation, but we cannot call them supernatural, but rather speculative; and if we are not fortunate in getting them solved, we do no harm in leaving them that some one may enrich his character by giving evidence of very high attainments by doing in the future what has not been done up to the present. There are many curious statements advanced—some of which you can have no means at hand to disprove or confirm. This great sight must necessarily have its greatness and sublimity enhanced by weaving round it a network of fabulous and refined romance which is calculated to please for the brief space of time foreigners are held under its influence.

We are struck by the wild whirl and incessant storm and fury which rages on the upper rapids for a mile or so before the water reaches the Falls. If a storm of wind were raging we could pass on it and consider that there was an apparent cause for the effect which was passing before our eyes; but when all is silent, and nature, so far as the eye can see, is wrapt in the deepest repose, the impression is strange and unaccountable in the highest degree. We are told that the flood at the top of the rapids has a speed of seven miles an hour, which increases at the bottom to thirty miles an hour. Now, whether this is the real or only the approximate speed it matters not, as it shows what is the true cause which produces such a fierce and frantic war in this avalanche of water before it makes the last and terrible leap into the groaning vortex of the abyss below; and this wild commotion is imparted to a certain extent to the air, and in the stillest day one can always count on a gentle breeze round the margin of Goat Island and in hot weather this makes the island and the lake sources of desirable enjoyment. I have already referred to the storm which rages at the bottom of the Falls. Such a large and solid body falling from such a height is capable of moving everything which intercepts its progress, and against which it strikes, and it is said the rocks in close proximity to the great Fall are sensibly affected, and vibrate by the action of the water. I was disposed to test this part of the marvellous, and with this view I got out to the very margin of the great Fall from the side next to Goat Island, and held my ear and cheek against a rock for some time, but I failed to discover the faintest vibration on the rock from the stroke of the water at the base. I think that the configuration of the rock below is such that no blow takes place except at any time a fall of the rock occurs, and even then it is doubtful, on account of the channel and the great depth below. The depth immediately below the great Fall is greater than the height of the Table Rock above, and the momentum which is imparted to the water does not appear on the surface at all, for the water on the surface is comparatively at rest, and its course is slow; while the waters below must be hurrying through the channel at the rate of ten or twelve miles an hour. The proof of this is obvious, in the fact that all floatable substances rarely appear at the basin of the Fall, but are held by the velocity of the stream below and are carried down at once to the Whirlpool Rapids, where they are sometimes churned for a long time before they are swept down towards Lake Ontario, and it is very strange they should appear at this point, for the water is said, or supposed to be several hundred feet deep; but in the vicinity of this part of the river the water must receive a check by some great impediment—some obstacle—as throwing the water up with so much velocity as to throw it high into the air, and this at a distance of three miles; this phenomenon is seen down the St. Lawrence as well, and it looks like the action of shallow water, but the powerful effect it has on the steamer disabuses the mind at once of its being so. Some time ago there was at the Horse Shoe Fall a tower which was used by the curious to overlook the Falls, and a capital view and impression of its grandeur and majesty were obtained, but it was removed not long ago, as fears were entertained regarding its safety. It was not sufficiently near to the water to be influenced by its action, but in the winter time, when thousands of tons of ice are driven down the river, its stability might have undergone some change which may have induced the proprietor to demolish it entirely, and thereby avert any accident.

It is said that many have felt a strong inclination to leap into the flood while gazing into its vortex from some of the heights. This looks a strange story, and unaccountable in the extreme, but such a feeling as that might come to the surface in some persons whose constitution disposed them in a particular direction. I tried the experiment under the fascinating influence and advantages which teem around the most attractive spots, but cannot say that I felt disposed in the remotest to distinguish myself by any such impressive piece of daring. I had no longings for the fame of those who dream of securing it by such a startling method. I daresay in reference to this wonderful statement many would be inclined to stand on the order of their going and fail to go at once. Accidents, however, are rife at this spot. To make a false step here is tantamount to making a fatal one; for it is difficult to extricate one's self at any point where such a slip takes place. I did not take notice whether there was any means at hand for the rescue of a person overtaken by accident. I rather think there is none. I do not remember seeing a life-buoy, ladder, or anything of that sort. Perhaps these on past occasions have been found of no use, or they may be disposed to afford facilities for carrying out the prophetical tradition of the Indians, who have set down the number of sacrifices to the giant flood at the rate of two in the year. Whether this prophecy applied to Indians or not I cannot say, but about an average of one in the year suffices, but whether in fulfilment of the prophecy I leave others to determine or discover. I did not feel inclined to follow the Indian into his fastnesses, retreats, or solitudes, in the search of what I thought would scarcely repay the trouble. It is said, however, that the Indians have on certain occasions come from their distant settlements to look on this great flood, the knowledge of whose existence has been transmitted from father to son, and on these occasions they have sought the flood, and with serious, grave and reverend awe and religious ceremony offered a calumet (peakemu or pipe) to the Great Spirit or Kitchi Manetoua, as a thankoffering for their prosperous journey and safe return. It is a rare thing to see an Indian in the vicinity of the Falls. The Chippewa and the Iroquois are often spoken about but to meet one rather a long journey requires to be undertaken before their habitations are overtaken, but both in the town of Niagara and the village of Clifton there are museums where their works are exposed for sale, and a great trade must be done in them if one were to judge from the number of shops or stores which offer the various kinds of Indian work of art to the tourist or traveller as a memento of their visit to the famed spot. The Anglo-Saxon race are almost in possession of the whole country around, and one rarely meets an inhabitant of any other country who is a permanent settler. The town of Niagara has a population of about 3000. The place is very much scattered, and any grouping of the buildings in the form of streets has scarcely the effect of causing one to feel that a street is intended by the arrangement. Buildings of some magnitude are found in close juxtaposition with others which are foreign to them in style and use. But possibly all this distraction in the external features of the place may be taken or reckoned as imparting to it a charm, as it takes away the commercial character from the appearance of the place which is associated usually with places which have their square and compact elements carefully attended to. The hotels are a feature in the place. Of course here, where the commercial population is small, the hotels are not used as they are in great centres of the States as the dwellings of the bulk of commercial men; they are solely for the use of the moveable and fluctuating population. Tourists are public property whenever they come to visit places like the Falls; they are the peculiar care of the various auxiliaries belonging to the hotels, who are like your shadow, or the ever-present sound of the water which encircles you all the time of your sojourn. You are never left for a moment without their kindly influence being exerted over you. Whether it is that they fear that you may become a prey to that mystical fascination and power which are attributed

to these mysterious Falls, and that you may transfer
yourself, were you left alone, to their attractive and
fatal embraces. I know not, but their attentions are of
a fervid generous, and self abnegating character,
which is calculated to puzzle you as to where it has
its source. It would be uncharitable to suppose that
the knowledge of your being the repository of a certain number of dollars could induce such kindly
feeling, and genial and frank solicitude with which
you are overpowered. It is quite evident that the
chief of the business in connection with the place
has its origin in the thousands who are continually
coming and going to visit the world's wonder, the
hotels always being able to accommodate several
thousands. It is not possible to say which is best,
for where there is so much competition doubtless the
effort to please the customer will correspond. Any
number of vehicles, carriages, or buggies are in the
streets and openings belonging to the hotels and to
persons having no connection with them, and one
will be sure to be advised to have nothing to do with
isolated and wandering pedlars on the streets. I do
not say that their commercial morality is of a higher
type than the proprietors of the hotels, but I would
only advise any stranger who wishes the assistance
of these useful characters to believe the one as much
as the other. Anything I say refers to the United
States side chiefly, but I presume the hotel opera of

the river will not prevent the contagion from spreading to the other; but what I said in regard to the proprietors of the foreshore on the United States' side, must influence every one in their estimate of the people on that side. Any person or people who can, for the doubtful gain secured by it, shut out one of nature's grandest and most sublime and majestic sights, for the sake of making a profit of it, should be sent down over the Whirlpool Rapids in the winter time on a block of ice, and the Government which would allow such a transparent and despicable piece of swindling is not entitled to any generous expression of sympathy from any person of sense or considerate judgment. A British subject who has travelled so many thousand miles to see this grand and imposing spectacle, and who has approached it by way of the States, and finds he must get on British soil again by crossing to the Canadian side before he can see it, if he has any soul at all must entertain an intensified degree of supreme and just contempt for those who would make this full and sublimely grand voice of God equal to a trumpery show which is dragged by the scum of creation from town to town for the pennies or cents drawn from the curious.

The museums I referred to, and which are most numerous on the American side, are evidently worthy of being visited by all who go that way; but it is needless for me or any one else to suggest this. The person who can escape them by being indifferent to the solicitation and importunities of the keepers has all the qualities of a person who should make the round of the States. These stores, shops, or museums are chiefly in the places where strangers most do congregate and are of course a leading feature. We presume the daytime has been exhausted by seeking and enjoying the fair spots in the surrounding country, the after-dinner speeches have all been delivered and the deep shadows of an autumnal evening have settled down on and concealed all the beauties of this fairyland, and you walk abroad eager to inhale the cool and invigorating air or the sweet odour from the new mown hay; but to do this you must leave the air which permeates the entourage of your hotel and you pass on not knowing whether you go. By and by, you are attracted by an excess of light from one quarter, and as there is a cheerful look you are induced to proceed in that way, but you have not gone far without doing what is natural in the circumstances, taking a peep at the beauties which are spread in the window for the benefit of an admiring and discerning public; and while you are admiring the contents of the window you are politely told by two or three attractive young ladies that the attractions of the window are infinitely inferior to what are to be seen inside. You attempt to weigh this announcement in the balance, but before you have time to adjust the scales you are found standing in the interior of the museum, and it takes an effort of philosophy to enable you to discover the agency by which the transfer was effected so rapidly, and it is only after you have departed with your hat and coat pockets stuffed with the various varieties and your purse commensurately empty, that the secret dawns upon you in all its vivid reality. It is surprising the amount of business and talk which can be effected by these ladies in a night, and in some instances they will deliver an embellished statement with as much *sang froid* as if it was a plain unvarnished fact, substantiated by the concrete and respectable testimony of the local legislature.

A walk abroad in the evening round the great centre of attraction is impressive and grand beyond conception. The evening is quiet and calm, and all nature has glided softly into warm and luscious repose. The stars have fretted the deep blue sky, and they are scattering their rays of living light across the gloom. No breath of air disturbs even the tender branches. You look across the great chasm and you feel as if a spirit passed before you. High overhead it hovers, winged as it were with motion from below, rising gently and awfully, it stands a pillar of cloud by night, fenced round by the eternal music from the void beneath, fit emblem of immortality and life. We could forgive the untutored Indian if we learned that he had made this spot a temple for the Great Spirit to dwell in and receive his homage and worship, for at times there is much in and around it to excite and call out feelings of veneration and reverence, and impart the beholder with every attribute of his nature which lifts him from the gross and sensual accompaniments of this life to one of a higher and lasting character.

The streets of Niagara are very homely and rustic in their appearance, as if they were only recently reclaimed from the common with a sprinkling of shrubs and trees here and there, for the sake of variety, and variety is certainly not awanting in every corner of it. Here you find a mill, with the canal gliding past, giving indubitable evidence that it has been superseded by some more useful work, the antique bridge and the pathway across, where caution and circumspection are necessary to keep you out of the dangerous deep below. The ample and capacious hotel, surrounded with well-kept walks and luxuriant wide-spread trees, whose shadows are grateful in the mid-day sun, and close by the humble wooden building and the thrifty tradesman's shop, with broad brimmed awning to keep his stock safe from sun or rain. There is a special interest associated with the country here, on account of it being the scene of several battles between the old authorities and the new. This is the line which divides the States from Canada, and being the frontier a bold and natural line of demarcation—at times the war raged around the district between Fort Erie at one end of the river and Fort Niagara at the end next to Lake Ontario; and at many places along both banks engagements and conflicts have occurred between the Indians, Americans and British, and on the lakes also deadly strife has been often waged, when the great conflict or struggle for independence was going on. But now no military are seen anywhere, the Custom-house officer being the only Government official one has occasion to meet; and I daresay every peaceable citizen hopes that the bold and stubborn cliffs on the banks of the Lower Niagara, and its broad and deep water above, will be sufficient for all the purposes of division and protection, and that in all time to come the storm which formerly tore and severed the two countries will be hushed for ever, and nothing more formidable will appear to divide them than the impetuous stream of the Niagara.

CHAPTER XIII.

EN ROUTE FOR THE CAPITAL OF UPPER CANADA

THE kindly offices which one experiences at the Falls are not limited to the time you may reside there. They are also of a prospective character. How do you like our country? is a question which is ever and anon propounded, and following that, as a corollary, Where do you go next? Up to this time I had not travelled in the manner which is customary or common in the States. Tourists usually in the States, with consummate forethought sketch the entire ground which they intend to occupy in their projected voyages and at one of the many places where the sale of tickets takes place, they secure a long string of them corresponding with the desired route, and after that no further purchases are necessary, and by this arrangement a considerable saving is effected. You may get from ten to twenty tickets as the case may be, according to the number of places you intend to stop at or to visit, and when you arrive you hand the conductor the ticket bearing the name of the place, and you can stay there for any time, and afterwards pursue your way to the next place indicated on your coupon. And the advantage of such a system is of a highly commendable kind, as it saves all further anxiety about the purchase of tickets, and your undivided attention can be given to your baggage as you pursue your journey. At this point I was recommended and induced to proceed in the manner I have referred to. I bought my long string of coupons, which entitled me to bed, board, and passage by steamer and rail for the remainder of my route. These tickets or coupons are sold at offices often a long way from the station at which you intend to embark, and you have only to step into the train on arriving at the station and proceed, without even showing your ticket, which, if you happen to be a little late, is a convenience which you feel much in such circumstances. There are two routes by which you can reach Canada from the Falls, by rail straight across by London or Paris, and the other by rail and steamer to York, the old name of Toronto. This latter I selected, embarked, and found our track lay along the eastern bank of the Niagara river. The day was clear and fine, and our course was at times along the very brink of its high embankment, affording us facilities for seeing the bold and rocky escarpment on the opposite bank, and the jutting shelves with their rich fringes of variously coloured vegetation, the towering pines spotting the wild, irregular, and rugged stony palisades behind. Here, some huge and towering cliff seemed poised in mid air as if ready to take a headlong plunge into the seething flood careering between the barriers below; and there trees rise over trees, clothing the sides of the giant walls from base to cope. High into the air rose the pile of this majestic temple with its sides of rich and natural decoration, disclosing here and there its massive and magnificent architecture, chiseled by the hand of Time, and below the voice of the spirit of the flood rang up its eternal chorus, filling the entire chasm with its never-dying anthem. But shortly the train changes direction, and makes a detour further on, and we pass by cultivated fields, whose treasures here lie gleaned, and ready to store before the advent of winter with its stern and biting blasts and storms. The run is not long a long one, for shortly we halt, and the contents of the train are transferred to steamer at Lewiston, by a number of vehicles, which may be wanting in elegance but not in variety. A momentary bustle takes place and the horses and his rider are on their way again to Niagara amidst a cloud of dust, and with the lively admonitorations of the whip or the tongue to the propelling power, we move along jauntily for about two miles and our party is gained. The steamer lies at a wharf, and here we descend the embankment from a considerable but gentle a succession of steps, requiring both care and skill to do so successfully and safely. When the living freight has settled into its place and the various traps and baggage are adjusted, we cut our connection with the land, and move further into the stream, which lies like a still broad sea of glass, reflecting the foliage around its margin. Lewiston begins to recede. The big wheels are beating back the green water into snowy ripples, and the fresh breeze beats the grateful awning which spans the deck into life and vigour. The gorge of Niagara narrows in the distance, and the banks rise up like ramparts on either side, robed in their mantles of varied tints, mellowed by the autumnal sun. Queenston is passed, and the wide ocean of Ontario floats across the river's mouth, and on one side Fort Niagara looks over its water with its hundred loopholes, and from the flagstaff swings the flaunting "Stars and Stripes." We touch at the opposite shore at a small place on the Canadian side, and now we are on Lake Ontario. Our next port is Toronto, and for the next few hours we are surrounded by the waste of water, and our attention and curiosity must be directed to the steamer and its contents, or reflections of the past, the imposing sights we have left behind, of the magnitude of everything in the country, which attracts attention. Its lakes, its rivers, are unending, infinite; its bays are oceans; its caves are the portals to the blackness of darkness, teaming with stalactite and stalagmite wonders and beauties, the chambers of which, for number and intricacy, are beyond human power to explore. Numbers of them have been illuminated with glades for the curious to see their interior, but the real of their ramifications have not been seen yet. There are falls twice the height of Niagara, but the body of the water is not so impressively grand and awe inspiring. There are small lakes of unsurpassed beauty with scenery surrounding much like our Tsu-cha. There are mountainous districts, but these are not so grand. They do not breathe of immortality, nor point in the direction of the soul's aspirations. They are not mantled in romantic life and grandeur nor crowned with snowy or cloudy coronets. They do not reach to the distinction which grace those mountains that have their embattlements high in the clorius and artillery of the upper world, and round whose top the spirit of man communes with the sublime and beautiful in nature.

We have gained the middle of the lake, and the land we left behind has sunk below the horizon and the shore in the direction of our port leaving to rise up as from the deep, on the left nothing is seen but a thin thread marking the line where the sky and sea meet, while to the right hundreds of miles intervene between us and the land, and the different aspect of the surface makes one feel as if the middle of the Atlantic was our position. There is not a single sail in sight crossing this trackless and sublime ocean

We near the land, and are struck with the marked character of this side of the lake, or rather this part. The high table-land or the rampart-like bold shore is only on the side we have left, and on the Toronto shore the land is flat and level so far as we see from our ship. A long spit, tongue, or hook-like island lies along in front of Toronto Bay, and extends for miles, serving the purposes of a breakwater, and must be serviceable to the port when storms drive the waters of the lake in that direction. There seemed to me to be a difficulty navigating the steamer in crossing this bar, and sundry " ports " and " starboards " curvettings, backings and forwardings, are necessary to catch the line of the channel, but shortly we round the bay and get into the wharf or quay, and the bursting vapour from the steam pipe trumpets our arrival at the capital of Upper Canada, and I have made my first trip on an American lake. I have purposely omitted to say anything about the quality or character of the steamers, as I will have an opportunity to do so after a while, when I get on one of the other lakes, as steamships on this are not equal to those on the States lakes and rivers. They serve the purpose as well for what they are intended, but they are plain and commonplace; while those in the trade referred to are miracles of marine architecture.

Toronto has a foreshore in extent similar to Greenock,

about two miles or so, and on or along this space are many public works and evidences of a thriving city. The wharves are many and piles of all kinds of stuffs are crowding the available landings. The pier where we landed was packed with a heterogeneous compilation of everything, and to escape from its intricacies required both time and considerable labour. At this pier the manner in which we could leave her passengers, and those who intend to prosecute the voyage to its end take another steamer which goes down the Saint Lawrence to Montreal —thirty hours' sail or so among the Thousand Islands and over the rapids. But as I wished to see part of the Canadian interior and an acquaintance I transferred myself to the Grand Trunk Railway Station and got my luggage checked, intending to return the day following. My train did not start for an hour or so, and I had time to look about. The stations of this city reminded one of home. The Grand Trunk especially resembles the station of the Scottish Central at Perth. It is almost new and quite worthy of the great system it is connected with. On the lower side of it are the Luggage Offices, Ticket Offices, Parcels Ticket Office, Refreshment Rooms etc., Waiting Rooms, and Officials Apartments. And this is the only station I saw in America worthy of being called a station. The stations of the Great Western and Northern surpass the rest of the American stations, but the Grand Trunk is the Yan...

pareil, and is evidence of the new vigour, life and action which have been infused into this gigantic enterprise, which was disposed, on the part of its management, to take a nap by the way for a while, and settle down into a lethergic condition, when the zenith of success had been attained, or was supposed to be so. At first the entire system was constructed on the old or broad guage system, and I daresay a difficulty was experienced of extending operations, a transhipment of goods entailed expense, and limited the action to its own plant; but now that the guage is changed to the now almost universal standard, its fresh blood will receive scope for circulation over the great continent. To be able to run cars to and from Chicago, Montreal, Portland, and other large centres must necessarily give a stimulus to trade previously unknown. Everywhere the old rails have been taken up and the whole replaced with steel rails, new rolling stock has been created, between four and five hundred new engines have been constructed, new bridges, &c., and the £2,000,000 which the company have put into their hand will enable them before they are done to create the finest railway system in the world. And if there is any part of the world where such enterprise is needed, it is on this great British-American Continent, with its vast resources for enterprise and skill. In every direction the tide of emigration flows over the continent, and with a

railway system carrying freeh labour and the other
agencies necessary for the conquest and clearance of
the deep and interminable forests the difficulties of
immigration and colonisation are to a great extent
overcome and lessened, and great facilities afforded
for the advancement and execution of the laborious
work which awaits the colonist on his arrival. A
widespread and effective railway system is of the last
importance in any country, but especially in a country
where there are no old beaten tracks to guide the
steps of the new settler in his search for a new home.
It is especially so. The cars on this line are splendid
specimens of finished work of this kind. One would
suppose there was no need for anything like costly
and elaborate decorations on these cars but the
managements are determined to be abreast of the
times and it must to a certain extent be an inducement to the travelling public, and if it is not so, it is
a decided comfort to those who are obliged to travel
by day, and those who have to travel by night are
enabled to do so in a palace car, so to set down "a
palace car." As I said before there are both gorgeous
and elegant. At the customs they ask 1.25 for
the night trains and for two dollars you can enjoy
the felicity and comfort of a palace for the whole night.
In Canada the same principles of railway management as in the States are carried out. The Pullman
cars are not the property of the various lines on which

they are found, but belong to a company which pays for the privilege of running their cars over the lines of railways. And as I stated, the persons wishing to use the palace or sleeping cars get tickets from an official representing the company they belong to, and who at this station occupies an office of his own. The emigrant car is another institution. Of course we do not expect to see an attempt at anything like luxury in connection with these—they are plain and commonplace, like the cheapest means of conveyance in our own country. These are provided frequently as part of the contract with the emigrant before he or she quits fatherland. These are attached to all the trains, and ordinary or first-class is reserved for the travelling public. Whilst there is thus a general spirit of progress in relation to comfort and stability going on, a person from this country is rather astonished at the irregularity of the trains. Time is seldom or never kept, especially on lines where there is any extent of traffic; and if it were not that they were wrought with single lines collisions in all likelihood would be frequent, but the train which is first due at the siding station must wait till the train from the other direction comes up and passes, and thus trains are prevented from colliding, and the sacrifice of life is prevented at the sacrifice of time, the loss of which is least felt. The facilities which the rapid extension of railways give must be great to the commercial portion of the States and Canada in sending to produce to the ports, where it is embarked, and to central markets. In Canada railway extension is slow and cautiously projected; but in the States an almost opposite course is pursued. In the beginning of 1856 there were 35,000 miles of railway in the States in operation; and one-half of that amount was made during the preceding eleven years. In 1859 over 5,000 miles were made, and since that period nearly 8,000 miles have been made. In the first instance the lines are single, double lines being rarely used; and when we consider that the building of railways in America costs only about a third of what they cost in Britain, they ought to pay well, and the Americans think that their railways are better managed than they are in Britain, the fares are less, if we consider that first-class is the degree of travelling accommodation provided. In travelling in any part of the American continent folks from this part of the world are apt to forget that the time is not uniform there as it is here, the extent of the country being too great to enable them to adopt any such arrangement, and as the time is sometimes that of the city you have left, and at another time that to which you are going, you are perplexed, especially whilst you are on the move, and as the result of this your chronometer is never telling the truth, and confusion on the part of strangers is sure to be frequently manifested.

As this city is the chief centre of importance in Upper Canada, there is much that is interesting on account of its being so, but as my train does not allow me as much time as is necessary to see it at present, I will take the cars and reserve it for examination on my return from the interior. The trains are not numerous in the course of the day to any of the distant places, and they are mostly trains which are proceeding from Montreal or other places, such as Portland or Richmond, going west, and are joined by the cars from Toronto. The station of the Grand Trunk Line stands on the portion of the west-end of the city next or near the lake, and the cars here are brought along in the same manner as in many of the State cities through the central part of the busiest portion of the city, and enter the station at one end, and leave by the other.

The usual stillness which occurs between the trains is superseded by various movements indicative that the train is approaching, and the intending travellers are on the *qui vive*, baggage is all piled on traps ready for transfer to the officials in charge. The usual amount of steam whistling and creaking of compound breaks and buffers, and fitful and nervous vociferation take place, and hurried adieus are interchanged, and we are off to the West! On this line there are many stations which have familiar names, but on the whole they show the lands to have been settled on by people of various countries. The route as far as gone over by us, was flat and level; considerable tracks of it cleared and fully cultivated, others only partially so, and dotted with myriads of stumps, but without levegress. This was very generally the character of the country along this line, interspersed with a number of smart-looking villages the traits or features of which we will have an opportunity again of seeing. After a run of about four hours we arrived at the town of Berlin, Ontario, Upper Canada.

CHAPTER XIV.

BERLIN, UPPER CANADA.

When I arrived at Berlin the deep and impenetrable shadows of a Canadian evening had settled over the landscape, and I felt somewhat at a loss, for the station was some distance from the town, and the morally felicitous condition of this part of the "New World" did not necessitate the practice of lighting the public thoroughfares, and strangers have just to grope their way in the dark in the same manner as the settled portion of the population do. However, I was favoured with the casual guidance of some young folk who were returning from a fair held at the neighbouring town of Guelph, and these served the double purpose of company as well. It was not long after sunset, but the rapidity with which the day deepens into night after that luminary has sunk is very marked, and is beyond our idea in such matters; but when I approached what I took to be the town, from the number of windows which were strewing their glowing lights across the gloom, I made a halt, and on making inquiry I found I was standing at the side of the Presbyterian church,

which was at that moment occupied by my clerical
friend whom I was in quest of. I entered the porch,
and after a series of attempts in the dark to find a
passage, I at last succeeded, and took my seat in one
of the remotest pews in the church, and as there was
but a dim religious light, I managed to secure my
retreat to the end of the service without much
trouble.

There is nothing on earth which reminds one of
home and its highest associations more than that of
going into a church in a foreign land and finding the
same person officiating who had done so at home,
frequently in the same form and the same words, the
same sounds, the same "Lord's song in a foreign
land," when, perhaps, "Dundee's wild warbling
measures rise," or some one of "Zion's sweetest
lays." Then, by the magical omnipotence and speed
of thought one finds himself transported in memory
back through the wild and confused labyrinth of the
past and intervening scenes to his home far across
the floods. Such were some of my feelings between
the times of my entrance into and exit from that
House of God on that night, after having passed over
a considerable portion of the Canadian continent. If
I were to say that my friend was surprised and
pleased and pleased and astonished, to find a visitor
from "Auld Scotland" in the Canadian interior, I
would only tell you half of the truth. We were

times talk of "angels' visits," but scarcely in Canada have they such a thing, and when an occasion occurs they are inclined to regard the person as such; and then it is their aim to give one the proof of it before leaving them.

The distance we had to travel after leaving church was not great, and it would be a work of some magnitude to rehearse the thousand-and-one inquiries about home made by the Rev. Mr. Dickie, for midnight did not mitigate the demands which were made upon me. But as there was a new day coming, we both retired—the one confident of being able to supply the demand the other was likely to make upon him in reference to what was doing in the "Old World."

A night's repose brought the morning wreathed in dappled clouds of gray, chased with gold and ruby tints, and robust with the glow of youthful health. The light was frolicking among and along the tops of the distant pines, and on the cones of the metal covered spires, then back to the east again, when I walked abroad to see the town of Berlin for the first time. Of course it is unnecessary to say what part of the world the first settlers came from, and who made this their habitation and home, or though one, were it possible, were cast ashore on this part of Canada, he would not remain at a loss for any length of time as to the nationality of its people. The German

element is still strong but there are representatives
from many European countries, and we can easily
learn that the past was not remote when the foundations almost of this place was laid, for it has none of
the mellow and matured features about it. One can
easily conceive of the date of its being reclaimed
from the forest which surrounds it of which its area
formed a part. At that time it would be but a farm
in a wood very much like others which are more
recently formed. We cannot discover any natural
advantages which would induce any number of persons to fix on this spot as likely and suitable for a
town or city, but perhaps such a distinct aspect of
matters does not form an ingredient in the calcula-
tions of the early settler, and on a great continent
which is comparatively level there is not that same
scope for the exercise of the choice of the settler
but from the fact that it grows, and prospers materially, we must infer there are advantages of some
kind about it though these are only what are common to the whole country — the fertility of the soil.
The earth yields its increase with comparatively little
labour, and on honest stewards of care. There are in
Berlin some 3000 inhabitants and some ten or twelve
denominations, each having a place of worship which
may be designated a church, and this fact proves it
an active and, intellectually a very enterprising
community where there is much attention to the

growth of principles as well as agricultural produce
The ground generally is rich, and the industrious
and careful farmers are wealthy, because they work
hard, and are good husbandmen. Poverty is little
known there, not because there is an absence of
vice, but that is not so rampant, neither should it be
when there is the presence of so many temples. The
interchange of friendship and social sentiment is
liberally indulged in, and there is much geniality of
deportment evinced in the promiscuous intercourse of
everyday life; but one is weightily impressed with
the light and evanescent character and quality of
everything which surrounds him, or at least the bulk
of what he sees. The houses are wood; the slates are
wood. There are no dykes or walls except what are
wood. The pavements are wood, and the coal is
wood. But there are some of the well-to-do citizens
who live in *chateaux de brique* very tastefully constructed and embellished with what indicates wealth
and culture; but these are limited, though from the
signs of commercial life and energy they will be sure
to increase. There are some public works engaged in
the manufacture of such things as the possession of
plenty of wood gives facilities for producing, and they
are sent often far away over the continent. There
are great numbers of Dutch—industrious, wealthy,
and exemplary citzens. Their personal appearance
generally does not indicate wealth, but the opposite;

but their forms and tank accounts gave their personal appearances the like slicer. Quiet, sober, industrious, obliging, fraternally as in some things they band together to promote the united well-being of the whole. As their sentiments, commercially, socially, and religiously are one their notions are consequently the same in relation to the practical aspects or phases of their experience in adversity or prosperity. They are almost uniformly the followers of one form of religious belief, and follow it with the strictest and severest rigour. I don't know that their one form is limited to what pertains to the purely spiritual for with the inflexibility of fate they apply it to the cut and colour of their coats, and with unflinching and persistent aim and decision apply the restrictive injunctions to the number of buttons that ought to adorn that garment. They do not for a moment doubt that the general aim of Providence extend to the minutest fragment of what has its existence in his universal kingdom, but to make any effort to save a stray sinner, or a barn in a thunder-storm by insuring the one or the other would argue such an amount of infidelity as to debar them from being recipients of the consolations which are dispensed to those only who, shelling forth Pauls, go with soul and effort onward. They are successful farmers, their barns are broad and capacious, and rumour says of them sometimes that the carcase of a Turkey, or a York Chicken, and their own

is suggestive of the wealth which can be extracted from the land with comparatively little labour, for in many instances a very few hands suffice to labour the land. They have two temples in the community, and the disciples of Swedenborg have one, in which it is said their efforts at proselytising have been very successful. There are also Episcopalians, Lutherans, Roman Catholics, and Presbyterians. The hotels in this small place are almost as numerous as the churches. There are some eight or so, which is certainly a very fair supply, and shows that the number who patronise them on market days is large, or that here considerable numbers do not keep house of their own. Market days are frequent, and the stir in the place on these days is quite animating, and gives one a lively notion of the commercial character of the folks from the surrounding country. The stores are very ample, and give evidence that the prospective wants of the people are thoroughly understood and provided for in every department of creature comfort, and especially in the literary line, for one store contains a selection and number of books, which speaks highly for the intellectual calibre of the inhabitants who are the storekeeper's customers.

One would naturally suppose that where so many hotels are in existence, there would be a disposition on the part of the people to drink deep; if so, the

outward evidence of their having done so is not
apparent. Perhaps they do not feel inclined to carry
this proof of their libations into the public thoroughfares, for one rarely sees a person who is capable of
giving the same substantial and incontrovertible proofs
of his felicity as we are at times favoured with at
home; or perhaps the virtue of American stimulants
does not induce the same genial and felicitous constitution in man which we see in this country so frequently.
But I daresay there have been manifested at times
tendencies to lean in the opposite direction, for in
Berlin on Saturday nights the drinking places are
compelled to shut before seven o'clock, and this has
the effect of promoting a virtue which is cultivated
largely and which the Legislature intends to enforce
where there is any apparent laxity or disposition to
neglect it. I am not qualified to say anything in
reference to the public morality of the place, but one
would say, from the absence of anything like a staff
of officials whose business it is to check and restrain
the irregular passions and vices of the people, and the
absence of lights on the public streets, that there are
few who require the attention of those public servants
who in some places are on the alert night and day to
preserve the peace and promote a species of morality,
which is even commendable in the absence of a more
praiseworthy kind.

During my stay here I had the pleasure of enjoying the friendship of Sheriff Davidson of the place, and also Mr M'Dougall, the chief civil and judicial magistrates, both worthy representatives of the great power which emanates from the Home Government *via* Ottawa. But I am afraid, were I to say nothing more in regard to these gentlemen, I would require to sustain the oft and well-merited attacks of self-reproach; for when one has such friendship expressed, and in a manner which is the spontaneous effusion of an ingenuous, frank and generous nature, and by cordial and kindly expressions of unrestrained hospitality, we feel it is an important duty to acknowledge how it is appreciated, even though the disposition to do so is cramped by doing it through a public or partially public channel. I must say I feel a little pride in saying that both of these gentlemen are Scotchmen, and it is a little singular that those who are virtually the head of the executive in a place of German origin should be so. But these are not solitary examples in Canada, nor does Canada give the only examples of this kind. It would be of little or no use to say anything about the moral character of the place. The legislative functions operate always smoothly and sweetly where there are good subjects, and officials thoroughly qualified to administer the law, and give a vital exposition of law-abiding influences on the character. The country in the neighbourhood is not marked by any of the irregular and romantic beauties

which one would desire. It matters not in what
direction one looks—the same straight line of horizon
meets the eye, and then the forest, park, and the
snake-fence wriggles along the foreground, and back
into the forest again, and its zigzag features wind and
encircle the whole cultivated portions of the reclaimed
parts of the continent. There is a stream here and
there "rushing o'er its pebbled bed, imposing silence
with a stilly sound." There are no vast floods leaping
and sparkling from the rugged mountain side. There
are gulleys, rising grounds, and here and there a
snugly ensconced villa looks out from an enclosure of
fruit trees, bearing on their extended arms rich and
luscious fruit; and often there are tokens of the
weight they have to bear being too great. Frequently
the roadside is strewn with offerings of their prodiga-
lity; but rarely are they lifted, so profuse and cheap
are the bounties of Pomona and so little are they
regarded. I think the finest rowan tree I ever saw
was here. It looked almost one solid mass of red
from the upper to the lower branches, it was used as
an ornament in front of a villa, and was very marked
on account of the quantity of berries on it. Everything produced by the farmer can be bought for one
half the price which is paid for the same articles at
home, but despite the cheapness people are careful
and moderate in the use of them. There are evidences of the extension of trade—new lines of railway

are being laid. There is one line called the Doon Line, just finishing; but I cannot say whether it will run to Ayr or no, which is some 12 miles off. I wanted to see Ayr, and Mr Dickie and I took a cariole and posted off to see that Scotch colony, and a brother clergyman, Mr Thomson, formerly assistant in St Andrews, Greenock, and the drive was most enjoyable and sweet. When once fairly out the landmarks seem to be insufficient for navigation. Through and along the waste of woods the roads are wonderfully good in some places for a new country. Some portions have strongly marked corduroy, where a declivity gives the water facilities to tear it up during storms. Large tracks of land are under cultivation, and farm steadings on suitable spots. These steadings are mostly built of wood. Some are log huts, strong and comfortable within, but rough and homely without. A grist mill of considerable pretensions is perched on an ample and suitable neighbourhood, close by a village with a Dutch name—Amsterdam, I think. There are signs of activity about, and the incessant whir of machinery within gives faithful note of sturdy and honest thrift, and the miller in his well-powdered suit outside looks to the disposition of supplies. Another farm and then another forest—the road skirts the chequered allocation of the land—we pass the ruins of Aberdeen, the first city or the nucleus of the first city, planted by my friend the Sheriff in honour

of his natal city, when he first went to that far-off
land a youth, and when he used to pass a week in the
bush without seeing a living being but his dog. This
is the quality of the men who are wanted to enlarge
the forest and make it blossom like the rose—self-
reliant men, who are accustomed to think for themselves and act for themselves, and who do not stand
upon the order of doing, but do at once what their
hands find to do, whether it is to fell one of those
patriarchal giants in the wood or lay the foundation
of a log or clinker-built hut or house, rear the snow-
apple, the tomato or the tobacco plant; rear the vine,
potatoes or poultry, build a sawmill or hold the
plough.

But we have arrived at the hostelry of the old
Dutchman, a genuine type of the old roadside inn
of a hundred years ago. In some respects it resembles
that of Dirty Dick's in Shoreditch, but the Burgundy
is A1 at Lloyd's, and to pass without allowing old
kindly Mynheer to slake the thirst of our panting
Bucephalus would be ungracious, and some horses
do lose no sleep if one or he never *oblivion* comes
over ahead. The fountain is an indispensable adjunct
on a long road; it breaks the journey and renders
the hours pass; it shortens the way by lessening its monotony, and adds a new relish by change
of circumstances. Much, I daresay, could be said
in favour of these little houses into the straight

line of a highway even of a few hours' journey. We are nearing another village, but there is nothing which commands attention about it. We have seen many of the same kind before, and it is scarcely worth while looking at this. There is nothing in the name to indicate the race or the people who laid its foundations. They do not aspire to make themselves a great name in the world, and if it has name enough for their far-off friends to find them out, they have no higher aim to accomplish by it. But now on one side a deep ravine appears, and in the distance numerous human dwellings rise. " Is that the Doon that's rippling through the trees ?" I said. "No," said my friend, " but that is Ayr in front of us." I found, on a little inspection, that it was not on account of any —even the remotest—resemblance to the old that this new Ayr was so called, but from the names on the sign-boards one could understand that many of the people might have come from Ayr or other parts of Scotland. I cannot mind of any place in Scotland like to it; it is purely agricultural in all its aspects, and destined, I am afraid, from its position, never to surpass any other place in any one feature or enterprise. But its character and prospects may change in the event of the iron road passing through it, as has often been the case in Canada as well as in our own country. We transferred our locomotive power to the tender mercies of a homely and kindly-looking

equerry, and without any difficulty discovered the
home of the young pastor. Our visit was necessarily
brief, being only sufficiently long to enable us to
partake of a few of the comforts of a missionary's life
in Canada, and a vocal gem of the old country,
accompanied on the piano, by Mr Thomson, who is a
capital singer; and after a kindly adieu, we mounted
our buggy and retraced our way across the country to
Berlin.

CHAPTER XV.

GUELPH AND WATERLOO.

WHEN I first directed my steps to the novel, peaceful, and rural scenes of these Canadian lands, I had no idea of the penalty attached to thus breaking in upon the quiet and sunny repose of the people. I thought one had just to go and convince himself that such lands and prosperous abodes existed, and then when that was accomplished to give an indication of his mission being done, and pursue the uneven tenor of his way to other scenes yet unexplored. This is the manner in which a stranger would propose to do, not knowing the character of the people among whom he has fallen. To go and leave a place in Canada without seeing everybody in it, and every place around it, looks like only doing half the work; and to leave such a broad and liberal land without participating in its spontaneous and generous offerings, would be to leave with an unhallowed and unwarrantable conception of its people's character in all matters relating to the entertainment of strangers. I have already referred to the existence at this time of a Fair going on Guelph, 15 or 16 miles distant, and at such gatherings the whole resources and capabilities of the country are concentrated and exposed to show the progress which is going on in the country generally; and that such was to be seen was submitted as a sufficiently powerful reason why I should prolong the time of my sojourn, and go and see what could only be seen in Canada. The day was fine, and many were met with their faces toward the town of Guelph. The trains were crowded, having got well filled up on their way from the interior, and when they reached the station of Berlin, space was at a premium; but we got packed in a perpendicular position, and in a short time were transferred to our destination.

The town of Guelph occupies a rather pleasant position. It looks well from the cars as we pass along and rises gently on a hill a small hill, gradually sinking towards the back part of the town and rising again. The streets are wide and airy, but do not run at right angles, but are found to run in such directions as the configuration of the land renders necessary. There are some very nice buildings, banks, churches, and public offices; and among the ordinary specimens of domestic architecture there is unrivalled variety, which in a place of this kind, and as Guelph is, is very agreeable. Everything about it has the stamp of newness, and nothing seems to have subsided into the settled position of existence. We can tell to a day almost when this place dawned into being, for the first tree which was felled when a clearance was made of the forest where it now stands was felled by the hand of a great man—a man whose history is closely connected alike with Guelph and Greenock—I refer to John Galt, the novelist, who was appointed by the Canada Company to manage the sale of the Crown lands in Canada, and went out in 1824, and conducted that enterprise for some two years only, as he resigned the appointment in 1827, on account of some unfair representations made by the Governor of Canada to the Board of Directors in London. It is not too much to say that likely much of the popularity which the place has experienced is due to the selection of the place made by a person of such large experience and brilliant parts as Mr Galt proved himself to be prior to this date; and as an evidence of the high respect in which he was held by those associated with him in the important work he was engaged in, we may notice that the neighbouring town of Galt was named for him by his friend the Hon. William Dixon, after Mr. Galt had left the continent. There is very decided evidence of Guelph being a thriving, growing, and prosperous centre, from many prominent facts, which the state of the town during the fair supported. The town on our arrival presented a very animated and odd appearance. In some four or five of the most capacious streets were piled or filed, two or three deep, hundreds of buggies or carrioles on which the farmers in the vicinity of the place had come to the town. These of course were all empty and the horses in the stalls, and in many instances their owners in the hotels enjoying the respite from the early rise before going to the Exhibition Grounds. This was found to be imperative, as the grounds were a considerable way off, and it was best to take something substantial where one was sure of getting it.

The grounds were in the suburbs of the town, in a comparatively level field or succession of fields. There may have been several hundreds of acres. There seemed to be as much ground as Guelph used on and bestowed in rather a permanent character; possibly the ground was kept for the purpose of their annual exhibition. I was somewhat startled with the number of conveyances I saw on the streets at first, but when the number of people who were keeping holiday could be seen at a glance, one could very easily reckon that many had come by the trains as well, and that the vehicles, I think, only indicated those who possessed the land in the remoter places, where railway communication was difficult to get at. In the centre of the great space was erected a large wooden building; permanent too, I presume, for a wooden building there indicates permanency as much as a stone one would do here. It looked well suited for the purpose to which it was devoted. The centre was ample, and had galleries which were reached by several stairs, and the visitors promenaded these and could see all that was passing or going on in the lower part of the Rotunda, which was allocated for the exhibition of musical instruments, pianos, and melodians; and as there was always a profusion of sweet sounds ascending, hundreds were wont to bathe their senses by letting them creep into their ears. This part of the Exhibition was strangely foreign to the rest, which embraced everything connected with agriculture—Canadian agriculture. In the first department what referred to or was useful in laying the forest bare—the uprooting of trees, cutting, barking, fencing, draining, ploughing, hutting, digging, hoeing—in fine, everything which the primary condition of the land demands. And there were many beautiful specimens of agricultural machines and implements, and they were all the work of mechanics and artists in the province. Then, in the second place, there was the finished work—that which the husbandman had brought back rejoicing, the reward of his labour and his toil and his waiting in hope, and these were classed, and each had its place in one of four annexes which ran out from the central building, and divided something like this—the dairy, the garden, and the field, the first being devoted to agricultural implements as I have already noticed. In referring to the garden,

I may as well say that only the useful of that department was there. Flora brought no offering to that temple, but the pomological display was worthy of that goddess whose robes are always decked with luscious and goodly fruits, and whose smiles are lit up with sunbeams as she comes with her cornucopia replete with bounties from her fertile bowers.

It is not at all needful for me to specify the kinds of produce which occupied the benches. Everyone knows from what I have indicated, that mountains of all the good things of the earth were there in their most savoury and attractive form, but piles of butter and cheese alongside of piles of potatos looked a little incongruous and out of tune; but in places like this, where there are only statutory periods of bringing together the people and the various products of the country, we cannot expect to find a delicacy and refinement effecting the arrangement such as we see at home in exhibitions of any magnitude. In the field outside of the central building there was a magnificent display of everything which lives and moves and has its being on that part of the earth in connection with pastoral life. Field-work and poultry. Along the lane or enclosures of the enclosures were fixed and portable domiciles for the winged tribes, from a few inches to three or four feet in size, and the variety of kinds, colours and form were something bewildering, and were quite consonant with the babel of sounds with which they were striving to regale the crowds who were admiring their qualities. The classification of the kinds and sizes, to a very casual observer, was at once evident, and it was observable that in this part of the Exhibition to effect sales was as much aimed at as prize-taking, for numbers of the lots were specified as sold, and I presume that the commercial as well as the competitive feature applied to the entire round of the business of the field. It is not possible to detail the extent of all that was open for visitors, for every class of stock had a representative here, and would have afforded an opportunity to a person fully conversant with the subject to dilate on the merits or demerits of any one to his heart's content; but I cannot speak of what I saw with anything like authority, further than what may be regarded as an echo of the generally expressed voice of those who were presumably acquainted with what was going on. Nor were competition and business the only features of the field; while the older heads were engaged in what was likely to be a source of profit, the juvenile, the irrepressible and volatile exuberance of youth, had its side of the field allotted to it, and from which there was one continuous stream of screams of laughter and joyous sounds— hobby-horses, merry-go-rounds, and all the inspiring mechanism and attractions for the young mind in holiday times. On a wooden structure, above the

heads of the curious crowds of human beings, was
perched an instrumental band, discoursing music for
the pleasure of those who were enjoying the promenade in the open park, so that the sounds in the
field were as varied as the animals exposed in the open
air, or the products in the building. On the one side
we had the shrill and lively treble from the youthful
and jubilant crowds, and from the stalls we had the
fitful and occasional soprano and deep bass from the
full and tremulous bovine throats. On the other
parts of the grounds the judges were busy giving their
awards, whilst Taurus, in his impetuous temper, with
flaming eye and restless limb, scowled the inquisitive
critics from his side.

On the side of the field near to the entrance was a
wooden house of a very temporary character for the
sale of refreshments. Everything was there which
was likely to be wanted; but the cup which intoxi-
cates could not be found on the premises, and was
most unlikely to be found there, for the department
was altogether in the hands of the Young Men's
Christian Association of the town of Guelph, and
they had their colours nailed to the camp tent, shed,
or marquee, and a very imposing amount of business
was gone through by a considerable number of young
men and young ladies, who gave indubitable proofs
of their muscular Christianity by the fervid and unremitting application to the work that was ever-

whelming them at times. I may just remark in passing that this is an example which gives us the reason why these associations in America are so wealthy. It is surprising the property they possess in some places in the States especially, and we can see that a repetition of the labour such as I have referred to would place in a short time a considerable sum in their hands; for that is doubtless the object they have in view, so that they may carry out effectively the great work they have in connection with their organization, and in reference to which their labours before referred to are subsidiary and subordinate. When a person from this country mingles as I did on that occasion with such a multitude of human beings, and in the capacity of enjoyment seeking, he is disposed to think there is something out of joint, when he does not observe the almost universal symptoms of joyous activity and wild and frantic gesticulation and vociferation and clamorous tumult which accompany holiday observation at home. Although there was nothing intoxicating sold in the exhibition grounds, the hotels were accessible by all on that day, but despite the opportunities and facilities for getting the intoxicating cup I don't remember one case of drunkenness nor an approximation to it. I may say at the same time I am unable to submit a substantial reason for this state of things. We have the ocular proof, but whether in a scientific point we are to look at it in relation to social economics, natural philosophy or moral science, is a question which would require more than a few days' reading to enable them to solve sufficiently. It is, however, a gratifying matter to see that so many are able in new countries to secure enjoyment without having recourse to an undue amount of stimulants. I don't wish, however, that any one should suppose that because there were none of those noisy demonstrations observable, there was any want of enjoyment or the least evidence of that state of things. There was none of that stolid Teuton gravity to be seen, but a healthy and fresh expression of sensible enjoyment.

These exhibitions are continued during the fall of the year in the principal places in Canada that are great agricultural districts or centres, as Guelph, London, Paris, and other places which are suitable for effecting the purpose for which they are intended, and, as I have indicated they are of a double character—the promotion generally of agricultural interests, by affording facilities of more extended culture of land and cattle and for enjoyment and competition. I do not know that the Canadian Government gives such facilities for the promotion of agriculture as is done in the United States. On the other hand, I did not ascertain that in the States such great central fairs were held for this purpose as in Canada. In the States, by means of the Bureau of Agriculture at the

City of Washington, the fullest facilities are afforded to farmers in every part of the Union by means of statistics published at the Government printing offices, and at the Government expense, in relation to every branch of agricultural industry, and reference to matters which can get no prominence at fairs, and such as can only be discussed in serials that are sent out to the remotest parts of the States, and bearing on all phases of land labour. On leaving the grounds very many took advantage of the means provided by a host of eager and voluble car-drivers, who rightly judged that a few hours' round in the park was likely to tire the most indefatigable, and necessitate his transportation to the town in some other way than walking. And the scene at the gate was remarkably animated, and we felt that a change of attitude or posture would restore the equilibrium of our motive power, but nothing beyond that, for the entire equipage savoured of rustic simplicity to a degree that could only be equalled in some remote spot in the country. But to aim at anything of a more exalted type would have shown an error in the circumstances, and our inability to adapt ourselves to the inevitable condition of the time and place—an imperative duty imposed on all who would reckon themselves capable of taking their place by the side of those who are masters of the situation in Canada. They all stoop to conquer who come to this great land, and those who gain the mural crown are those who have made the greatest breach in the deep and broad forest wall which opposes them in their efforts to subjugate the land.

The condition of Guelph in the evening was what one would naturally expect—much hilarity and buoyancy of spirits manifested by the junior portion of those who were engaged in pleasure seeking. During the day I was under the guidance, direction, and control of my young clerical friend, and our friend Sheriff Davidson whom we casually met in Guelph, thought that I should transfer myself to his care for a portion of the evening, as he was sure I would not be liable to the same privation that I was doubtless exposed to on the previous part of the day, for he thought the quality of the hospitality of Le Jeune Hotoor would necessarily be strained, and he was anxious that I should be relieved from any unfavourable tendency in that direction. There was much stir at the hotels, much talk, no doubt, about the success or failure of competitors; but as it was just about sunset when we left, I am unable to say anything of the aspect of things at a late hour. There were hurryings to and fro. The station was crowded by many like ourselves, awaiting for the first train, for there is an earnest and deliberate effort made to have the day's work done by the time the shades of evening close around them. But by that time we were on our way to our destination, and in a short time we were at the station at Berlin, and were accompanied home by a similarly lively throng as I had seen on the night of my first arrival. These fairs create a considerable stir and excitement in the country, for as soon as the one is finished the other begins. I cannot mind whether it was the fair at London, Hamilton, or Paris, which was next in order; but the fair succeeding that at Guelph must have been considered of more importance, as one train which passed up had one or more immigrant cars filled with Indians who were on their way to expose their wares for sale. There was nothing of the kind at Guelph exposed in the central building, which was the only suitable place for doing so. If the pianos were the production of a house in Guelph, then there was nothing at the exhibition but the production of the district. I know there is a warehouse in the town, and most likely they are made there; and if so there might have been a reason for excluding work such as the Indians bring in for sale, not for competition.

On the west of Berlin there is a little and likewise a thriving place called Waterloo. The road from Berlin to it is very good, and there are some good houses, possessed by gentlemen who have their business in Waterloo or Berlin. The central portion of the place is compact, and has some good shops well stored. I had arranged with the Sheriff to drive over the most interesting portion of this part of the country, and we devoted Saturday afternoon to the purpose. On our arrival at the town or village we had an opportunity of discovering several interesting features that had I less observed I would not have seen. The first object of interest we were asked to explore was on the north storey of one of the simplest shops or stores in the place, which was furnished with a succession of rows of rocks which bore the characteristic marks of having come from the south of France, and whose age and excellence were worthy the attention of anyone even like what we saw. We satisfied ourselves that the mineral was what it was represented to be, and thus satisfied, we called back to see the plains of Waterloo. I had seen great tracts of good timber lots but the land by which we passed was the finest I had seen in Canada. Here and there the picture of a house formed for thick and compact background and between it and ourselves lay thousands of acres of land well cultivated, well-fenced, and in many instances well-drained fields, but their crops had all been dotted with an occasional field of timber corn here and there. Sometimes we remarked along the very edge of the impenetrable wood, hundred of miles deep, with tall trees even, up to the sky, and the silence of which is something fearful and one could hear a stray cow's bell tinkling for miles off. These bells are hung round their necks, so that they can be found in the woods, should they chance to go in that direction, and are the only means of discovering the cattle should they stray far from their accustomed haunts. All the crops are stored inside; there is nothing left out, and hence the necessity for those immense barns one continually sees surrounding the farm steadings. The roads were all good over the entire route.

The houses were chiefly wood, whether they are farm steadings or ordinary dwellings. The principal apartments in ordinary dwellings have no fireplace, and when the weather necessitates the introduction of the stoves, they are set down in any part of a room; and the pipes are placed in such a manner that by running them through the roof they heat all the apartments upstairs in houses of more than one flat, and sometimes the pipes pass along the length of a room before they enter the apartment above, and by this means the whole heat is utilised, and the entire house heated by one fire. The air in the country here has nearly the same quality as it has at home. When one has moved along in it for a few hours it inspires him with a disposition to think of the felicitous relationship that exists between such healthy enjoyment and the gastronomical attractions

of the dinner table, and when we arrived at Forrest-
hill, the chateau of Sheriff Davidson, we gave his
good lady tangible proofs of how much we had
enjoyed our visit to the village and plains of
Waterloo.

CHAPTER XVI.

TORONTO AND THE LAKE OF A THOUSAND ISLANDS.

As I have already stated, my object in going into the interior of Upper Canada was just to take a fleeting and transitory glance at this land and the life of its people, and, so to speak, return with the next train; but, instead, I managed to spend four days or so replete with every sort of warm and kindly inducement calculated to make my stay longer. But there are times when one finds it necessary to make a strong effort to disengage himself from the potent and subtle influence which even kindness exercises over time; and though it entails a considerable amount of pain, it is only "like," as Sterne has it, "a cut across the finger," sharp and decisive, and immediately time begins to promote the cure. There is no doubt that the parting of friends interferes for the time with the consolidated amount of pleasure derived from their society; but a person on the move has greater facilities of shaking himself free of that than one who cannot enjoy the varying changes which tend so much to secure it. The parting at a Canadian railway station, I dare say, proves often to be a very protracted affair, on account of what I have already

stated in connection with the irregularity of the trains.
It was so in my case, and what a painful business to
keep two young ladies and along with them a bachelor
of divinity for one whole hour, looking at the "waifs
and strays" which are seen in the vicinity of such
places. But it is endless at last, for the arrival of
the iron horse cuts short all interludes—a brief
salient, one step from the platform to the car, a fitful
puff and a scream, and away we are landed to the
Upper Canadian capital again.

When the train arrives in Toronto in time, there is a
choice accorded the traveller whether he will go by
steamer or proceed by the Grand Trunk in the evening
to Kingston or Montreal. Primarily it was my intention to take the steamer and sail through Lake Ontario,
and then down the St. Lawrence, but as my train was
an hour behind, I had the felicity of seeing my steamer
in the offing by the time I got to the pier, and by
such misadventure I got a few hours to look at
Toronto, and I was not sorry of it after all, as the
evening train overtakes the steamer at Kingston at six
on the following morning, and it is only at that point
the Lake of the Thousand Islands begins; and now,
having ascertained my own position in relation to
our steamers and time, I direct my steps in the
direction of the "Queen's," which looks out upon the
expansive lake with its imposing array of sunshine,
and where all loyal subjects of Victoria are treated

and refreshed in a happy, homely, and courteous manner by one who was at one time a denizen of Greenock, and where, hesitating whether I should first enter or view the city, I was deprived of settling on my own account, for at that instant I was met by Mr M'Dougall, from Berlin, who had preceded me in the early train, and who insisted I should occupy his apartments at the " Queen's," and be his guest till the train in the evening started. To this proposal I could not hesitate; and I accepted it in the very spirit in which it was made. So far as I could see or judge, the arrangements at this hotel were very similar to what they are in the States. The house is large, and had been increased lately, and I think is the first in the city. After practically testing the quality and the amenities of the *table d'hote*, Mr M'Dougall, another gentleman and myself, *un tiers d'ecossais*, sallied out to see the lions of the city. There was much to see and little time to overtake the whole, but, with the assistance of a charioteer who knew the city well, we got over the most interesting sights before the shades of evening descended on us.

As I indicated before Toronto stands on a low lying *plateau*, which extends in a pretty uniform level as far as the rampant-like land in a line with the mouth of the Niagara river, some thirty miles or so; and a very marked and obvious distinction exists between the land in these localities. In looking out upon the

lake you feel as if the land and water were upon the
same level, and any rise or elevation in the city is
very gentle and scarcely recognisable as one moves
along. So far as my memory serves me the same
tendency which exists in all towns and cities is
observable here. The bulk of business is conducted
and carried on in the east, and the west end is appropriated for sites of handsome mansions, public institutions, and ground for various kinds of recreation.
In the east are some very splendid public offices and
warehouses of stone, brick, and granite; and the business aspect of the locality is calculated to remind
you of some of our large cities at home, for some of
the buildings might take position or stand comparison
with some of the Glasgow public offices, and in these
localities there are the incessant stir and bustle which
you see in similar places at home.

The main street and some of the chief streets
running from it are flanked by some very fine
buildings, and some of the shops are equal to those
of Buchanan Street in Glasgow, but these are by no
means numerous, and they are idly posted between
and in the vicinity of others which give them all the
effect which they merit on account of their architectural elegance and superior finish and attractions. The
general aspect of the place is Scotch, and when the
usual stir is in the streets, and numbers promenading
the public thoroughfares, and the tramway cars going,

one feels as if he were walking in some Scotch town. But in the suburbs it is not so; there is an admixture of the Scotch, Canadian, and American noticeable in the streets and villas. The wooden pavements, public walks, disposition of the grounds, and the arborial surroundings and the general amenities of the whole, are not strictly consonant with what one sees in the interior, and hence one is led to infer that the business spirit which moves and regulates the weightier matters of the place is Scotch, and the subordinate are a mixture, representative of the countries named. The public buildings are all worthy of being noticed— I mean the exterior—and I doubt not but the interiors are not belied by what is seen on the outside crust. I had not an opportunity of seeing many, but these may safely be taken as an indication of the quality of the others. The chief or principal of these are beautiful specimens of the styles of architecture they represent, and the spires of some are highly ornamental to the city, being floriated Gothic, and light in their construction. I do not think it necessary to mark out any one, for there is certainly a combination of merit which induces one to think or suppose that nothing but a commendable spirit of competition could have effected so much to speak of the public spirit and enterprise of the inhabitants of the place.

The Post Office is a plain, capacious, and substantial building, and must have been in existence for some years, and has all the appearance of being capable of carrying on the business of the city for many years to come and the general character of it was evidence of the decided enterprise of the place, and in a business point compared favourably with other places I had visited in relation to this branch of public enterprise; for in Washington, Philadelphia, Baltimore, New York and Montreal, there were new Post Offices in course of erection, and all magnificent buildings, but none of the old Post Offices were equal to the Post Office in Toronto, and this fact, I think, indicates a spirit of enterprise ahead of the places I have named.

The principal building in Toronto is the University, a new and massive public building situated in the Queen's Park to the extreme west of the city, and promises ample facilities for students of law, physic or divinity. The site is one worthy of the College, and the building is worthy of the site, but the staircase, class-rooms and lecture halls are soundly lighted with a dim and inefficient light giving the whole interior a very dull and questionable look. The museum, which is yet in embryo, promises to supply a want which is of great importance to the artistes in a new country and to the intelligent as a piece of intellectual recreation. The grounds which surround the University are ample, well laid out and studded with a fine array of trees. The avenues are entitled to be called magnificent; the grounds being level, and the trees being placed and disposed with great care, give them a look similar to those at Hampton Court or Windsor Avenue. In a prominent part of the park there is a statue of the Queen, an indispensable feature in all Canadian places of any magnitude, for British Americans cannot suffer that their loyalty should be questioned for a moment, and it is sometimes amusing to note and hear their expressions of devotion to the Crown. This applies to the Upper Canadian districts; in the lower there are so many subjects of a foreign potentate that a neutralising effect is produced in the hearty expressions of their loyalty, and this state of things may be found indispensible *pour preserver la paix.*

Toronto is the seat of the Superior Law Courts, and these are concentrated in Osgood Hall, a substantial stone building not far from one of the entrances to Queen's Park. It is Grecian in style of architecture, and is enclosed by an iron railing, and surrounded with gardens of some extent and tastefully kept. I was a little surprised on entering to find indications of what I had failed to discover in the majority of American places. The interior of the hall or court was a succession of what one might expect in the Law Court in the British Metropolis. The interior architecture of the building was a material manifestation of a determination to make the city a centre, distinguished by many types of what has its existence in the old country. One could scarcely believe he was in a building in upper Canada. There were wide and capacious staircases, balconies, and landings, with majestic pillars supporting elaborately decorated friezes, capitals, and cupolas, with parapet and screens and richly stained-glass windows. Walls hung with the portraits of numerous members of the bar, and snowy-headed judges who had passed from the scene of their labours. The libraries were extensive, and the rooms were large and replete with everything that would indicate advancement and comfort. The officials were respectably attired, and the older heads looked grave and severe, and there was an aristocratic air of importance and respectability pervading the whole official life and trappings of the Courts. The place wore a quiet aspect at the time we visited it, but there were no symptoms to show that our visit was in the least annoying to any of the gentlemen of the bar.

In one part of the city there is a structure which is quite unique and inspires a stranger at his first glance at it, with a disposition to inquire as to its use. It is quite a specimen of rustic architecture, and is used for al fresco concerts during the summer season. It is built wholly of the wood of young trees with the bark left on, and is arranged in all the fantastic ways in which it is possible to put it together. The band and the audience are inside of this, which protects them from the heat, and the openings allow the gentle breezes to distil through them and cool the listeners within. The grounds all round are planted with a fine display of all kinds of flowers, and the space for promenading is considerable, and what with the music from the inside of this curiously planned Indian temple, and the various attractions to the eye without, the visitors must enjoy themselves during their stay, while the concert season lasts. The ground here was rather limited in extent, for there was nothing beyond that of a public garden intended. The park which I have already referred to being the most suitable for any imposing public demonstration. Indeed, all American cities are provided with ample public parks, and the extent of many is nearly equal to the Phœnix Park in Dublin, and on this point there is evidently an obvious aim at competition going on in the cities of the New World.

I cannot venture on one single remark in reference to this city in a social point, for by the time we had driven round and glanced at what I have referred to, the quiet grey sober shades of evening were settling fast, and we were obliged to make our hotel the next point of interest, and this I found very indispensable previous to undertaking a long journey by rail. Mr M'Dougall and I were just seated when we were joined by Mr Alexander Mackenzie, a well known Scotchman and who was at this time leader of the Opposition in the Canadian Parliament, and who has since become the Premier of the Dominion of Canada. I was very glad to make the acquaintance of a brother countryman who had distinguished himself and raised himself to such an eminent position. He seems to carry his honours easily, like every patriot who has devoted a lifetime in the interests of the land of his adoption. After leaving the "Queens" and bidding good-bye to my Berlin friend, I had the pleasure of having some conversation with this Scotch Canadian statesman at the Grand Trunk Railway Station, as we were both waiting the same train, which was an hour or more behind time. But it was not on the "North Pacific Scandal," or any of the great questions affecting the British American Dominion, but on the unenviable eminence which Scotland had attained in connection with drunkenness, and one can easily conceive that all well thinking and all well living Scotchmen abroad must feel deeply the stigma that is attaching to the land of their birth, and which is now almost passing into proverb. I had good reason for believing that the conversation was closely listened to by a person—who was the third I had seen to-day in America—stumbling rudely forward to let my companion know that he knew what he was. I cannot

v

say that the inebriate was a Scotchman. It is possible, however, that he was, and was anxious to give a glowing and fervid display of his national pride in the recognition and success of his countryman; but the strength and effervescence of his feelings and inspiration deprived him of the necessary and happy medium of speech, and possibly he thought that a still tongue would evince a greater amount of wisdom than any eloquence which he could command in his felicitous condition.

I have already referred to everything of interest in connection with the Grand Trunk Railway, and cannot recall anything worthy of notice which occurred between the capitol of Upper Canada and the little town of Kingston, where we arrived, after a run of over 160 miles, about half-an-hour before the steamer which left Toronto at mid-day the day before. At Kingston begins all that is attractive on the passage from Toronto to Montreal. This station is virtually the head of the lake of a thousand islands, and is as near as possible half-way between these places. The lake itself is a sight of intense interest on account of its fertility in rich romantic grandeur. Its pleasant and variegated scenery is the ideal of all that is grand in any part of creation. To pass through its fairy islands, by its limpid and rippling streams, over its surging and impetuous rapids, and its glassy bays; to look upon the sylvan

shores of the floating islands, with the verdant and
rich fringes of vegetation reflected on the crystal
waters as the steamer passes silently along the tortuous and serpentine avenues, whiles narrowing to
the breadth of the steamer, and sometimes expanding into the size of a tiny ocean, with their exciting
currents and boiling and rushing floods, afford a
succession of most desirable enjoyments on the passage down to the great outlet at the Island of Montreal.

When we arrived at Kingston the morning was
dull, grey, and cheerless; a mist was hanging around
the margin of the lake, and the westerly wind was
driving the surf over the pier, and the passengers
were crowded into a wooden box which did duty as
a waiting room, and the [...] was similar to
what one experiences on a Highland loch on a morning
with corresponding weather. A general gloom over-
cast the expression of the tourists, for as charming
weather transmutes the lake into a liquid paradise, so
does the reverse transmute the pleasure-seekers into
[...], but a broad bold gleam of golden light
burst through the clouds before we got well out of the
lake into the St. Lawrence stream; and by-and-bye
we were looking on the brilliancy of a fairy scene,
and the lovely panorama began to move and recede,
disclosing an unending succession of seemingly floating and varied islands, some clothed with compact

leafy, and shady bowers; some were tiny objects not much bigger than a good *pate de famille*, and others, rejoicing under the full culture of the farmer's skill. The banks were almost of a uniform height, and great trees marked the confines of the Yankees' territory. Broad and ample farms, the neat cottage, and the log hut alternately dotted the landscape, and now and again a tributary stream sent in its water to swell the floods. At intervals some one of the minor rapids was passed, gradually initiating the expectant and living freight of the steamer for the crowning effort of the skipper's skill to take his craft safely across *les grande rapides*. At almost every point in the river where rapids occur, on the banks there are canals for the safer passage of all kinds of vessels. Mills and public works of various kinds are here and there on the river's side, and by-and-bye we arrive at Ogdensburg, a place of some importance, with its railway connecting Lake Champlain with the St. Lawrence, and on the British banks of the river Prescott connects with Ottowa, and the Grand Trunk scours along close by the river on to Montreal. We have passed over several rapids, and as night begins to approach we arrive at a small French settlement called *Coteau du Lac*, where the steamer takes in a fresh supply of wood to keep up the steam; and we enter the canal and we learn that the captain cannot run the grand rapids. The water in the river is low, and the attempt would be hazardous and the attraction not worth the risk incurred. We try to console ourselves at the tea table and in any other refuge at command, and soon we commit ourselves to the quiet of the dormitories below, and glide into oblivion to the romantic air of

"Here, brother, oar, the stream runs fast
The rapids are near, but the daylight's past."

And when we awoke in the morning we were quietly moored alongside the quay at Montreal after a run to the distance of about forty hours from Toronto.

CHAPTER XVII.

THE CITY OF MONTREAL—LOWER CANADA.

ONE cannot approach this part of the country without having feelings akin to those which would naturally possess him were he *en route* to the Holy Land, and the nearer he approaches the more strongly does he feel that the first settlers were surely a people of sternly pious proclivities, for many of the places, and anything which necessitates the possession of a name, are named after some saint, whose family or existence nobody knows anything about. The places all along one short line of railway are called, without exception, after a whole string to them, and one does in spite of his better judgment feel as if he were in a rare atmosphere, and breathes, lives, and moves in an odour of peculiar sanctity. On some of the islands are to be seen, on those parts where the water is eternally lashing against, and naturally where danger is sure to overtake the incautious boatman, small crosses which, I presume, are intended to accomplish by virtue of superstitious means, what persons of greater success would secure by the adoption or application of scientific agencies. However, these are evidence of a dove-like and simple

faith which would be materially enhanced by an
addition of a little of the wisdom of the serpent.

The site of Montreal is one of great beauty and interest. The mountain, after which the island and
city are called, rises up and looks over the whole
land, with isolated and imposing dignity, and forms
a suitable and majestic background to a magnificent
city, where there are many splendid and gorgeous
temples and institutions, which bespeak the large
heartedness and liberality of the givers. On landing from the steamer in the morning I was not
favourably impressed by the first look I got of the
streets in the immediate vicinity of my landing
place. It was with difficulty one can come from
the steamer to the cab without going deep into the
sable mud with which the entire thoroughfare were
flooded, and from its universal presence around the
wharves it looked as if it were an indispensable
though uncomely covering to that part of the public
highways. After breakfast my first visit was to the
river side to get an idea of the extent of the trade at
the docks, harbours, or wharves, and as the sun had
risen with a burning heat, I felt a little cheery on
perceiving along the forest of quays for the fleet of
this black canal was sending up one continuous cloud
of vapour, and my consignee to it had in me compressor of as grave and dark an aspect as the mud
itself, and I thought the name suitable and sanitary

proceeding was to get away from its influence until the sun had absorbed these vile exhalations into a higher region.

The day was bright, and clear, and well suited for seeing the country, and in a short time, as I retreated from the river side, I found myself standing at the side entrance to the Cathedral of Notre Dame, and in a few minutes after on the top of one of its towers, from which a splendid view of the city and the vicinity is got; and if one can form an idea of the extent to which it is taken advantage of from the state or condition of the stairs, a very good revenue must be received. In the tower which is used for this purpose—for there are two—there is an immense bell of enormous vibratory power, and I think it has the dates of its birth and baptism recorded on it, but it is seldom used. The pinnacle of the temple is rather a dizzy height; but there are ample safeguards surrounding, so that one can sit and enjoy the extensive panorama with comfort and repose. The extent of the city can be seen at a glance—its palaces and towers, and the domes of churches, and convents. The Hotel Dieu, the princely mansions on the higher base of Mount Royal, the Reservoir, the terraces and spacious drives, the river and tributaries, scouring along in frantic ebullitions past the shipping at the harbour, the Victoria Tunnel, spanning the banks of the St. Law-

rence, and joining British America with the States
on the other side, and carrying the tide of commercial life across the opposite continent, from the
Atlantic side to the shores of the North Pacific.

The advantages which are possessed by Montreal
for the prosecution of a prosperous trade are seen at
once by any one who notes her geographical position, and the advantages of river and rail so that her
facilities are open, continuous and steady; and with
an active and enterprising population, her growth
and material prosperity should exceed the capital of
Lower Canada. There is incontrovertible evidence
of an amount of trade going on among the shipping,
but a city of nearly a hundred thousand inhabitants
necessitates a large trade for its own necessities. I
do not say that to the extent of its trade but a person going from manufacturing places like Glasgow and
Greenock, discovers a prevailing anxiety which
follows him into all the ramifications of his inquiries. It is not necessary for me to submit figures
in proof of what I say at present, but it won't require
a very acute effort of inductive philosophy to discover such before I finish my observations on this
place; but in the meantime, to begin, I may just say
that it is not many years since there was any
chance or hopes for the communication of the shipping carrying on trade with this city. This state of
things one would not wonder at so much had it been

in the hands of the French Canadians up to this time, but it has been in the hands of the British for over a hundred years—not virtually, but nomally, as any one will discover who knows anything of the history of the place; and after one notes the effects of the mild, temperate, and conciliatory polity extended to subjugated peoples or colonies, he is disposed to question its operation. Stagnation is evidently the tendency of the old spirit which once held undivided authority in the colony, and all the enterprise and vitality evinced by the genius of British skill and industry are exposed to the icy and torpid influence which it continually exerts. One sees its existence and feels it, and wonders that a people whose sympathies are antagonistic to the life of civil liberty are invested with equal political power, and allowed to use it, for the advancement of interests which are diametrically opposed in many respects to the best interests of the colony. I cannot do better than substantiate what I have referred to by a quotation from one who will be accepted as an authority of some weight. Macaulay, in speaking of the early influence of the Romam Catholic Church in connection with science and the arts of civilization, says, it was always favourable to civilization and good government from the time the barbarians overran the Western Empire to the time of the revival of letters; but from the time when printing was first called into existence to the present day the chief object of Rome has been to stunt the growth of the human mind. "Throughout Christendom whatever advance has been made in knowledge, in freedom, in wealth, and in the arts of life, has been made in spite of her, and has everywhere been in inverse proportion to her power. The loveliest and most fertile provinces in Europe have under her rule been sunk in poverty, in political servitude and intellectual torpor, while Protestant countries, once proverbial for sterility and barbarism, have been turned by skill and industry into gardens, and can boast of a long list of heroes, statesmen, philosophers, and poets. Whoever knowing what Italy and Scotland naturally are, and what four hundred years ago they actually were, shall now compare the country round Rome with the country round Edinburgh, will be able to form some judgment as to the tendency of Papal domination. The descent of Spain, once the first among monarchies, to the lowest depths of degradation, the elevation of Holland in spite of many natural disadvantages to the position which no commonwealth so small has ever reached, teach the same lesson. Whoever passes in Germany from a Roman Catholic to a Protestant principality, in Switzerland from a Roman Catholic to a Protestant canton, in Ireland from a Roman Catholic to a Protestant county, finds that he passes from a lower to a higher grade of civilisation. On the other side of the Atlantic the same les-

prevails. The Protestants of the United States have left far behind the Roman Catholics of Mexico, Peru and Brazil. The *Roman Catholics of Lower Canada remain inert, while the whole continent around them is in a ferment with Protestant activity and enterprise.* The French have doubtless shown an energy and an intelligence which, even, when misdirected, have justly entitled them to be called a great people. But this apparent exception when examinded will be found to confirm the rule, for in no country which is called Roman Catholic has the Roman Catholic Church during several generations possessed so little authority as in France."—Macaulay's History of England. I am not disposed to dilate on any of the aspects of civil government or their manifestation in the Colonies, but when one sees conciliatory and generous measures unproductive of their objects, it certainly justifies one in advocating measures of an opposite kind. When a nation possessing wealth, energy, intelligence, probity and courage, and the other qualities which fit it for conquest and civil government allow a subjugated people to retain and exercise all religious, civil and political privileges, and the jurisprudence of their own country intact, it shows a moderation which none of the great nations of antiquity ever aimed at or attained, and it is curious to note at this time that all the people or nations which have been deepest and truest in their

THE CITY OF MONTREAL.   237

devotion to the triple and towering crown are all
subjugated people, and without exception they are
all at a loss to see that any toleration has been
extended to them.

I thought the spire of Notre Dame a suitable
place to descant on the various points I have referred to with a large British city spread out before
me and so many convents, nunneries and institutions of a similar kind in view; and on the adjacent
tower a large gilded cross gleaming in the rays of the
morning sun, and from this — one could
judge of its being a favoured city, and one which
must be dear to the signal and final successor of Hil-
debrand, who is now virtually a prisoner in his own
territory. I was not disappointed in this, for when
I descended to the interior of the Cathedral, almost
the first object which attracted my attention was an
image of La Reine du Ciel with a young child in her
arms. The figures were cut in fine Carrara marble,
and a notice was in front stating that the group was
a present from Pio Nono ("Pius the Pio IX., 9th
April 1872,") and on a small label in front are the
words "afferrada a Sancta Virgen, et a Pio IX." Who
so impious and callous as to refrain from giving offer
such a chance of investing his or her offering, with
the double virtue of accruing to one or two of the
most important personages in the universe. I don't
remember noticing any such idyest of kindly recep-

nition and paternal affection to the devoted ones who meet in the Metropolitan, in the city of Dublin, whom I think his Holiness led us to believe filled the first place in his heart; but possibly they are all first in turn. One feels inclined to indulge in a little levity when observing or speaking of such things as one sees in such a place—shall I say in the House of God?—but when one sees as I did a simple girl coming in and bowing down and worshipping this calcareous idol, it is enough to make one ashamed of the genus to which he belongs who perpetrates such a fraud on the credulity of man or abet and encourage its perpetuity.

I love pictures when they are the product of genuine art, and when I stumble on an important church and expect to see something in the fine art line which will compensate me for the trouble of hunting them up, and seeing there were many in Notre Dame, I cast about for some one which might be of interest, and the first that caught my eye was peculiar, and it was on that account it did so. I have no wish to fleer and scout at any solemnity, but my judgment requires to be satisfied that there is solemnity in the matter before it will recognise the solemnity; that the picture was in a church was solemn, but anything beyond that I was not responsible for, and that it was regarded with higher feelings than solemnity I doubted not, for one young

THE CITY OF MONTREAL   239

lady who was genuflected before it seemed in an
agony of devotion. It was not very well painted,
and it could not be that it was an example of surpassing art which compelled her to assume the attitude of a poignant and deep devotion.

They who worship the one living and true God can
have but a very meagre and vague conception of the
convenience it must be to those who have a plurality
of deities to suit the complex and conflicting phases of
religious life and moral evils to which they are exposed;
and of the many intercessory steps and helps which
others, more highly favoured, have to enable them to
rise to the very summit of beatitude. One of these
steps was the picture I refer to. An embodiment—
as far as it is possible to embody in a picture—of a
dreamy, dogmatic swindle, the production of a body's
hypochondria and nervous debility, and who if her
superiors had sent to a *maison de fous* at the time,
might have proved the salvation of many who have
since lost the little brains they were possessed of, by
dreaming of pilgrimages to the piously romantic
locality of Paray le Monial. The picture I refer to
was not exactly the likeness of anything in the earth
or in the heaven above, and this fact may have
satisfied the very earnest worshipper—was she
conscious of it—of her relation to the first and
second commandments. The picture was intended
to represent "The man of Sorrows" and the

flesh of the breast was cut and rolled over, exposing the heart full to view, and the work argued the hand of an expert, so far as the cutting was concerned; and had it been done by *Shylock* he would have secured one of the conditions of his bond, for there was no evidence of a drop of blood having been lost; and the placid look in the face of the sufferer made the matter most incongruous, and gave it rather an amusing and serio-comic look, and how any sensitive young lady could make it an object of holy devotion might puzzle the venerable Margaret Mary herself. Perhaps a short extract from the writings of this venerable lady may give the reader a notion as to her sanity. The exercises are intended to be "offered by devout souls to the Sacred heart of Jesus." The manual is for the month of June, and the most curious and characteristic part is that for the thirty-first day of that month. But before I do so I will state the facts whereon is built the modern introduction of this doctrine or form of devotion. This lady says she saw "The heart of Jesus represented to her as on a throne formed of fire and flames, surrounded by rays more brilliant than the sun, and transparent as crystal. The wound which he received on the cross was clearly seen there. Around the Sacred Heart was a crown of thorns, and above it a cross which was planted in it," and this incongruous, ill-arranged, and unpoetically disposed mass of holy and sublime objects she is pleased to call a communication or "favour similar to that which was received by the beloved John, on the evening of the Last Supper." One is always learning. I was not aware of John having been the recipient of any similar communication, but the whole goes to prove what I have asserted, that the lady was once perjured herself. It is scarcely necessary to give the statement from her writing which I spoke of at first; let it suffice; in unison with the above. I have extended my remarks to a greater length than I intended in connection with this subject and religious matters; but I do not think I have done more than others who have been in the same position and have treated of the same subjects; and I know there are some who are anxious to know what is going on in foreign countries in religious as well as secular affairs. In this building were many pictures of subordinate interest, chiefly of saints, which are made to stand as links between this and the life of the higher world, and which we must necessarily regard as so many material barriers between the human soul and God. Of course pictures, miracles, plays and miracles served important purposes in the middle or dark ages when both priests and people were alike uninformed and ignorant of anything beyond an admixture of traditional customs, and the influence too possibly often exercised over a gullible brood of men, but to me

R

these agencies or a part of them in existence in the nineteenth century should tend to make men keep more closely to the light, and conserve all institutions which are allied to it with the most jealous care.

As I will have to notice some things similar to what are here when I come to refer to the Church of the Jesuits, I will pass them in the meanwhile, and only give a passing notice of a number of stalls which are arranged along the sides of the church, *petites salles de la question,* usually called "confessionals," the appearance of which naturally induces one to think there must be an awful number of sinners in what I had—from the prominent features of the place—taken for a city of exemplary sanctity and intensely-marked pious tendencies; but if "the fear of hell's the hangman's whip to keep the wretch in order," it is possibly necessary that that wretch should indulge in some devilry to secure the revenues of the Church against declension and bankruptcy.

The Cathedral externally is a bold, broad, and massive example of early Gothic. On the façade there are no pretensions to architectural beauty, but there is a telling and imposing appearance, and from the symbols which are conspicuously placed on the structure, the unlettered can easily recognise the degree of its claims to ecclesiastical altitude. Its steps are continually the habitat of some aged and

infirm recipient of the bounty of the charitable, and
visitors of all classes are anxious to acquire some
lesson or knowledge by their visit. The situation
which it occupies is not the best for a house of its
pretensions, though there is an important square
fronting it. Its being placed too much to the one
side operates to a certain extent in not giving it its
due effect. It is built of granite, as nearly all the
public buildings and churches are, and many of the
shops and warehouses, which are very substantial and
have a solid and remarkably good appearance. In the
vicinity are several banks, and not far off they are
erecting a new post office worthy of the surroundings
or amenities of the locality. The square, as I said
before, is small, and it is approached by four or five
streets, which are all narrow, giving the city at that
point an antiquated appearance resembling some of the
Continental places which were constructed in times
when such a provision was necessary to check more
easily the incursion or attacks of hostile neighbours.

On leaving the Cathedral, I took my way to the
right along the street called after it I presume
"Notre Dame," and in a short time arrived at the
Law Courts. I saw it was a building of some importance, though it did not seem to be in an important
locality, neither did it seem to have the appearance,
avenues and issues in a condition which would argue
that one would be justified in accepting it for what it

was. The boundary between the street and the grounds in front of the building had no parapet to denote the building was completed, although there were indications that such was originally intended. A few stunted trees were planted on the space, and the footpath was evidently more the work of accident than any line of design. The same features of embryonic imperfection stamped and pervaded the whole interior of the courts and offices. There were apartments where the business arrangements for the courts were matured, and the whole judicial work was carried on and completed, but there was a very strongly defined difference between this building and the one I had seen at Toronto for similar purposes. Every place bore a plain and common-place appearance, as if a disposition was evinced to give accommodation only for necessary work being done; but any display of taste or any attempt to deprive the place of an offensively plain and impoverished look by the addition of some few decorations there was none. The constructive and decorative traits of this house were in strict and in severe consonance. There was no relief except that secured by the necessary openings such as a window or a door. I was fortunate in meeting a very civil and intelligent officer of court, who was desirous that I should see everything in the courts which would be of service to me in getting a just and accurate idea of this department of the public service. I was shown the various offices or bureaux where the preliminary official work was adjusted before it came before the court; and all the offices had their official functions and distinctions indicated on or over the doors, both in English and in French, showing that the business of the courts was rather of a complex character, and necessitating in the case of many of the officials the possession of both languages, for, as I indicated before, the codes of both countries are used in the courts, not only similar laws, but the laws of the empire in their entirety, *la Code Napoleon*, as it is used at the capital of France, and the practice they call *La Coutume de Paris*. In the library I saw nothing which would remind one of the Advocates Library in Edinburgh. The room throughout was ample and airy; the bookcases were scarcely worthy of the name. The books were there, and my friend was anxious that I should see the chief among French law literature, which I have referred to above, but after turning over about a cartload of bulky and somewhat antiquated volumes, he gave up the enterprise, as they were likely on duty elsewhere.

All who are connected with the service and practice of law in Montreal know and feel that their position and labours are curtailed and crampled by conflicting interests with which they are surrounded. And in making inquiries at any friend in reference to the general appearance of things in and outside of the courts, his reply was, "We cannot have matters adjusted and set in strict consonance with British notion of those matters, so long as the present slow coach style of the original colonials exists, but British enterprise is beating back that old system of inaction and stagnation, and bye and bye we will appear in as advantageous circumstances as our neighbours;" and I presume, as a substantial proof of what he said, he took me to an old law court in one of the streets leading to the river side, where business—now done in the other courts—was carried on at a not very remote date, and there was certainly potent evidence of considerable advancement. And yet there is room for improvement in the same direction. In this street, which ought to be one of some importance, there is a monument of Lord Nelson, and from its appearance one would be disposed to think it had passed through the stormy days of Wolff or Montcalm, but I did not see any memorials of these heroes. The public market of the city stands not far from this street, and my friend kindly took me to see it. It must be—as its appearance would indicate—of a number of years standing; and at that time its stalls and benches may have afforded indubitable evidence of the necessity of such an institution, but from its present appearance one could not trustfully use it as a strong argument in favour of a similar structure in any city, for the old stereotyped forms of doing business either in the street or market are being superseded by the adoption of new forms which accord more with the tide of progress which flows continuously, and is permeating the remotest corners, even where the pulses of commercial vitality do not indicate that vigour which is felt in great centres of business. I thought it could not be to impress me with the great strides they were making that he had taken me to see indications of commercial famine passing in empty stalls as was the case in the market, but perchance it was not the time of day to see its usual superlative activity. I could see no traces of recent life in stir, and I considered the then present aspect and condition of affairs were the diagnosis of a chronic state, which prognosticated at no distant date its final dissolution.

Our next step was in the direction of the Champ de Mars, noticing as we went along some of the old buildings which have character to the old part of the city, and the great improvement which was going on. The Champ de Mars is situated not far from the square I have mentioned in front of the Cathedral, and as the ground falls leoli on the south and on the north side of the square, a good view of the situation of drill ground can be got from this eminence. In connection with the ground there is a drill hall and the necessary armouries connected, but the hall has never been completed, the roof collapsed and fell in on account of the weight, so that the first war to which it had any relation was one between the contractor and the official trustees of the building, and it is now an interesting and not very ornamental ruin. However, it is to be hoped that peace will soon be declared between the combatants, and that the young volunteer army may have a comfortable *rendezvous* during the severe and biting blasts of a Canadian winter. My British Canadian friend left me here, and pointing to his house up in the vicinity of Sir Hew Allan's, said—" If you are up the hill so far, look in if you have time," and "If I can be of any further service to you, my office is nearly opposite the Courts, where you can find me." He gave me his name, I gave him my thanks for his kind offers, and pursued my inquiries in a solitary mood. There are times when one can appreciate the kindness of such a friend, the spontaneous and courteous act enhances its worth and fixes it indelibly on the memory, and it even looks a green and fresh spot which one always sees in his retrospect on the way of life.

I had no thought prior to this of visiting the eminence on which the house of the merchant prince I have named was situated, as it seemed a task of some magnitude to accomplish, but I thought possibly it would repay the trouble on account of its commanding position; and as the day was far spent I saw there was an imperative necessity of doing so with all my might and enlisting additional facilities, and in a short time I found myself gaining a high social position for up-hill is the west-end the Belgravia of Montreal. After climbing the first step of the hill there is a fine level plain, and on this upper level are the homes of the upper ten. It is really a charming spot, the streets, avenues, and lanes are ways of pleasantness; the dwellings are embowered with the rich, shadowy verdure of sylvan attire, and are striking in an architectural point. The great bulk of them are of recent structure and great taste has been evinced in their adornments, and the prospect from many of them must be something grand. The drive along these avenues, with here and there an opening looking down upon the city, the river and the distant outline of hill on the States territory, the domes, spires, and minerets capped in metallic lustre and throwing the rays of the declining sun in every direction is exceedingly pleasant. Higher up are magnificent châteaux of the first merchants in the city and chief is Sir Hugh Allan nestling in the hillside—for the hill is covered to its very summit with luxuriant foliage, and all the houses have a cozy and comfortable look. Running up to these houses are subordinate avenues called possibly after the owners and I noticed many Scotch names amongst them, and so far as I could learn there are few of the original settlers who have risen to any eminence at all. The upper part may be regarded as the new city of Montreal. There is nothing to denote that it was taken possession of and used for human dwelling till a recent date, for all the buildings have a fresh and modern look about them. I have noticed that this city is the seat of a Roman Catholic See, and it is also the seat of an Episcopal See, and the Cathedral occupies a very fine site on the high grounds which I have referred to. The church is built in the Gothic style of architecture, which seems a favourite style from the number of churches built in it, and is finely finished internally and externally. The Church of St. Andrews is also a very fine specimen of the same style of architecture.

There are several colleges in the city, and the latest addition is a large and imposing pile of building, on a fine situation, and is the latest acquisition to the already numerous edifices belonging to the Catholic Church. The evidences of wealth in Montreal in connection with this Church must strike every one who visits there, and will necessarily lead one who is not previously aware of the fact, to enquire, where the revenue is derived from; and the answer to his enquiries would virtually explain many more, and some which I have referred to. The island is practically the property of the order of St Sulpice, the seignory or lordship being held by this order, and I think it extends to the island of Lachine also; and when we consider that the island of Montreal is thirty miles in length and ten in width, and its prosperity during the last thirty years or so by British industry, skill and enterprise, we can easily see that the revenues of that order must be great. I have noted a few curious things, but this last seems to me to be the greatest, and shows that our possession of the colony is at least a firm, and the winding of Lord Dufferin or any representative a most silly and impotent act of civil administration in connection with it.

The isolated position of Montreal operates against it in one important economy in nature—that of the water supply. Instead of the water running down from hills over the city, it is found necessary to force it up by its own momentum at the Lachine rapids a few miles above the city, possibly by the same sort of mechanism which is used at the village of Clifton at Niagara, where a powerful hydraulic pump forces the water to such a position or elevation as affords a supply to the village; so at Montreal the water is forced up to a considerable height to provide for the population. Some of the houses, however, are higher than the highest reservoirs, and it is likely they will require to find them a supply by private appliances. The tourist now pursues the path of his inquiries or observations the more in his movement and estimate of the beauty of the place, and the suitableness for a place of abode. The surroundings of the city as seen from one of the many points on the Highlands are interesting to a degree, and are calculated to attract one to do more than admire them. To a person who had time at his disposal to exhaust what is attractive and full of interest, much pleasure and instruction would be derived. There is much on account of the natural configuration of the land around to please a hurried and casual visitor, and though one might discern blemishes here and there in a wealthy and prosperous city, yet, if we know the reason of their existence, the reason being known might dissipate any unfavourable view or any ungenerous strictures one would be disposed to make. I had seen many of the churches as I passed along the avenues of the upper city; many fine villas, with their tasteful amenities; many happy-looking homes, fitly set in rich arcadian bowers, with the warm, mellow tints of a glowing sunset sparkling on the trembling foliage, and then the pallid and passive shadows of the night began to gather and descend and deepen into night. I left the Canadian Olympus, and descending the hill, I stopped at the entrance of the Church of the Jesuits, and stepped into the interior. There was just enough of light to show the tall gothic pillars rising and losing themselves in the vaulted roof, and to show to good effect the triple globes of fire hanging in their awful and mysterious orbits over the unseen altar below. In the church there was the stillness of the grave, broken only with occasional whispers from a number of statue-like erect figures, which were dimly noticed here and there in the pews, and from a number of human voices engaged as vespers in one of the adjoining halls, and the soft cadences of the music were floating in gentle eddies through the aisles, and dying in the recesses of the lofty roofs.

I thought I saw one or more apertures of Scripture subjects in low relief on the walls over the side altars, and I was groping my way to get the ocular proof of what I found I was mistaken in, when an acolyte made his appearance on the scene, and materially improved our wondrous condition by lighting up a resplendent blaze of gas behind one of the pillars in front of the altar. The effect was to a certain extent marvellous but like many or all marvels had its solution in art. I looked behind the pillar, and there was a reflector of great power, which threw the light with an intensity on the altar, and produced an effect which, coming after the previous darkness was quite magical in its effect. The garniture of the altar was elegantly constructed and arranged, there were ornaments of lustrous materials that made it rather extensive and sparkling, and was evidently intended as a point of interest in the church from the oddities and odd of its decorations. After putting the other lights in the vicinity of the altar adjusted, he carried in a small cabinet not so big as a davenport, and set it on the altar, and after doing so it was with difficulty he managed to complete his remaining duties, for ever as he passed in front of *La petite Boite* his legs seem unwilling to do their friendly offices and support him, and those who were present, I daresay, were apprehensive of the necessity of helping him out of his difficulty, but so long as I waited he was found to recover with the same alacrity as he evinced in his spasmodic attacks. I was inclined to think there was some electricity passing across his path from the suddenness of the interruption to his locomotion. But I could see no material evidence in support of this hypothesis; and I could ascribe his sudden inability and recovery to nothing but a miracle, as one is compelled to recognise the supremely divine and glorified texture of the piety of this brotherhood, for *toute puissance leur est donnée en les cieux et sur la terre* And we ought in all reason to be satisfied when we see any act which in its general features carries the stamp of omnipotence. That it is their misfortune of being unable to convince the world that they possess it, is really no proof that they do not possess it. And when we consider the invaluable services which have been rendered to mankind by them we can see it is only fair that some tangible and incontrovertible proof of their labour should be possessed by them. We can easily conceive that a disciple of such a worthy father as Pew Ignatov would often do many things which would astonish mankind, when we recur to his own wonderful art of begging his way from Montmartre to Rome with a bag of gold in his possession; few men could do so unless they were the children of such a father. And for the children it were easier to tell what they have not done than what they have done, their acts are so astoundingly unique, and numerous, some one says, I think, of one of them, "that he discovered that the moon was round and that the earth was square," and they had discovered the source of the Nile, of which nobody has been able to make himself a worthy successor, in going and doing likewise. They have become, in almost every country, the reflex of everything which is pure and holy and lovely and of good report, and men were forced to regard them as the very type of what was grand in morals and divinely exhaulted in the spiritual life, and men were unable to understand the disinterestedness of their motives, and disposed of attaining to the purity and sublimity of their piety and virtue. That they have not been rewarded for their labour of love in the world, it is scarcely needful for any one to say, who knows their history, or the smallest fragment of it. That men should find fault with them for affording facilities for defrauding robbing or cheating their fellow men was simply unkind and equally ungracious. That they should be cheated, cheated and vexed by those possessed of political power and influence, and not allowed to foment strife and hatch conspiracies for the destruction of empires is very inconsiderate and cruel. Why should that power be curtailed or limited which once dictated terms and conditions to the imperial omnipotence of the Western Empire, and why should these lambs of such Quixotic piety be made the mark for vile and unhallowed denunciations, and made to float in the defiled and polluted stream of the common life of the world. That we should see them enjoy some repose in Montreal, is quite natural, when we consider the nature of the soil and quality of the climate—it is always on the richest trees the most dangerous insects are found, and in fair lands churchmen will live in sanctified beggary rather than leave them. In Spain, at no very distant date, there was one churchman for every twenty of the population; but instead of its being a Paradise, it has become a morgue or charnel house for the bones of the discordant civil suicide; and fair Italy with its superior climate and a population, whereof three-fifths know nothing of the rudiments of education, is scarcely much better; and I daresay were it not for British enterprise, industry and skill we might be necessitated to record by this time the same state of things in this fair city.

I have noted several things connected with this place which show distinctively the existence of jarring interests, but one which catches the eye of a stranger as soon as any, is that of calling streets by the names which can be recognised by both peoples safely, as meaning the same thing—to have on one corner Rue St. Jacques and St. James. It looks like a work of supererogation. Of course I can say nothing in reference to the history of such a seemingly peculiar practice, any further than it is noticeable that it is not carried uniformly out. There are some streets which have only their name in one language, and these are not confined to the English nor to the French. However, it is likely these streets were originally called by French names, and when the English took possession of the place they thought it would be best to name them in the vernacular of both nations. In the part of the city which may be regarded as the oldest, the streets are very narrow, and these streets which are the busiest, and where the greatest amount of business is done, are not of a uniform breadth—but that is a feature which is often noticed in many of the old streets in many of our own towns and cities—and there seems to be no care or attention devoted to any of the streets which are not leading streets or main arteries of the city. I have referred to one square, which is considered the chief in the city, and the thoroughfares around it are in a passable condition; but when one passes the least to one side or the other, in proportion to the distance from that centre which one may go, he finds their condition gradually getting worse. There is another square which ought to be the first in importance, if one might judge from its being selected as the site for the statue of the Queen, but the amenities do not evince such to be the case. Perhaps it would not do to have a statue of the British Sovereign in front of *Notre Dame.* Its appearance there might remind them often of their bondage, and possibly it showed greater discretion to put it in a minor position, however much it might reflect on those whose influence ought to have secured for it the best site in the city; but, possibly, they may have a prospective idea of surrounding it with works of a nobler character than any which are in the more central square. That may be, but this state of matters is very faintly shadowed in anything we can see in the present outline. The only indication of it is in the fact that the street which runs up from the river at this point is the widest, and will ultimately, I should suppose, be the finest in the city. Again, the statue is on the direct line from the street to the chief or principal approach to the new or upper city, which may be in the future of great advantage in the way of being an offset to it; but it is scarcely possible to obscure, by picturing all the felicitous combinations of the future, its present ungainly and chaotic features. One feels as if an obvious attempt were made to give a bold and well-defined expression in reference to royalty, which should be an ample contrast with what is expressed by the people in the upper part of the continent. Inside an enclosure of not many yards in extent, surrounded by a fence of the rudest and simplest kind, and scantily adorned by stunted trees and shrubs stands a statue of the Queen of an empire on which the sun never sets, and this is in a city of possibly 120,000 people. One feels as if some artist had been making a miniature model of something grand, and had put it outside, that the people in the public highway might give their verdict in reference to it as a work of art. But we can only regard it as a faithful exposition of the extent or growth of loyalty in this part of her Majesty's dominions till the present time, but which will ultimately attain gigantic proportions, when the vile nightmare which paralysis free and spontaneous action, and all kinds of commercial enterprise, shall have received its quietus. The condition of the streets in the immediate neighbourhood is frightful and present quite a rustic appearance. This is not possibly what the Civic Legislature intended, for somehow when liberal provision is made for certain civic improvements, some magnate thinks the money would be better expended in some other way, and so far as I could learn something of this sort was discovered in relation to these public works or improvements. I do not say but some strange notion may at times take possession of heads which at any time are not very clear, and which are furnished with one idea only. It was said that one of the city legislators, who was chairman of the Road Committee, and who had more than a special interest in the Society of the Jesuits, was affected with a kind of distemper which brought the chief of the Tammany Ring to grief. And on that account the appearance of the streets and roads did not commensurately tally with the amount of money which was sunk in that enterprise. It is difficult to understand how such laxity in the practical or operant functions of a local legislator could for any time pass without recognition, but we are aware such have been, and overcame some men like a summer cloud, only to elicit their special wonder when too late. In large cities where there is much material prosperity by the growth of commercial pursuits, and especially in a city like Montreal, favoured by the presence of an order of men, who may regard all this prosperity and wealth as the result of their presence in the land. Then, how natural should it be for some part of the civic funds to be appropriated to secure a continuance of those blessings by providing the means to secure their invocations and friendly sympathies in time to come; and I think, in accordance with the *monita secreta* of the society, it is not necessary that they should tell the whole world

when any member is disposed to give them "a lift,"
as an expression of his impulsive piety. Their light
is of that complexion that it does not do to set it on
a candlestick, but propose lose under a bushel.

Among the many things which show a decided
contrast in Canada to the United States is that of the
expense of living. In the United States there are
many grades from the best to the worst class of hotels,
as there are in all places, but I cannot say that I
tested them in that respect, but as I found them,
without any special reference to their excellence as I
speak of them, and I may say that the difference,
taking my first and last hotels for example or
examples my fare in the States was thrice as expensive as that in Montreal. This may be the result of
one or two things, or of both. I do not think there
is the same amount of good eatables in Canada as is
in the States, and all kinds of the necessaries of life
are much cheaper, clothing alone being the exception. I had no means of noting any difference which
existed between the Upper and Lower Provinces of the
Dominion in regard to living. I had occasion to note
the prices of various things in the interior, which were
nearly a third cheaper than what we are paying for
the same articles at home and ample facilities are
afforded to any who are desirous to live cheaply and
"gather gear," — young folks especially who have
vigour and stamina to resist the inflernce of a Cana-

dian winter. Those who have had some experience of the climate say that good living, that is, having plenty of wholesome food to eat, is the best thing they know of for resisting the influence of the cold in Canada, and as living in Canada is cheap it may not be a formidable matter to one who is fortified after the manner referred to; and to assist what I referred to for the inner man there are cheap furs, moccassins, and the addition of a sleigh in the winter time I believe make life very enjoyable.

I don't remember being in any place where the streets were so quiet in the evening as they were in Montreal. I am not able to submit any positive reason for this state of things. One naturally expects to see a very considerable concourse of people moving about, especially on a fine evening. Such was not the case in some of the most important streets, and, I presume, it was not so in any of the subordinate ones. I daresay there are few such associations as we have at home which tend to crowd the streets at night by young men going and coming to and from their places of meeting, such as Templars, and very many kindred and benevolent and social institutions. I suppose there must be a want of inducement to bring the youth out at night. The young ladies, of course, are chiefly shut up in convents and nunneries, and the young gentlemen must sit at home and console themselves in the solution of some problem connected with social science or some one of the many speculative phases of experimental philosophy in relation to the arts of life, or be engaged in some of the enjoyments or employments which do not necessitate their appearance on the public thoroughfares or in the open-air. It is a little singular. I could have understood it in the upper part of the city, but in the vicinity of hotels and other places where there is usually a considerable amount of stir and activity it seemed to me somewhat unaccountable; but I have no doubt had my stay in the place extended over a few days, I should have come away possessed of the reasons of such a state of things in such an important city; and I am resolved that this and a number of other things which I find I have omitted, and which would have been of considerable interest to know, shall receive my careful inquiries, and scrutiny on the very first occasion I have to visit the attractive and prosperous city of Montreal.

CHAPTER XVIII.

EN ROUTE FOR THE STATES BY LAKE CHAMPLAIN.

"TIME and tide wait for no man," and in recognition of the evolution of this important and philosophic maxim, I arranged with the necessary official to "call me early," as I had resolved to quit the Canadian continent and prosecute my journey on to the States' side of the St. Lawrence on the succeeding day; and having settled my liabilities and climbed to an upper chamber where I was sure to get the first and freshest rays of morning light on their way to our sphere, I waited for the morning. The voice of my dreaming ear was scarcely attuned to any of the flitting sounds which trembled on its chords during the silence of the night, when it was startled from visionary into genuine and real consciousness by some one knocking at my door; and it was only when thus disturbed that I found how needful it was to negociate for it on the previous night, for had I wakened accidentally I would have certainly failed to look at my chronometer, for my window was only sufficient to allow but a very few rays to reach my dormitory, and from the dim grey twilight I would have inferred there was no reason for hurrying. But as it was I found I had sufficient time for my toilet, and shortly after a 'bus with a solitary passenger was seen wending its way along a narrow street where one would suppose "two wheel-barrows would tremble when they met," to the Montreal and Plattsburg Railway. The station was quiet and the passengers were few but somewhat strange, the bulk of them were negroes, which must have been unusual, for I don't remember seeing a single "darkie" on my excursions through the city, for they hold pretty tenaciously to the Southern portion of the continent, and so far north one only expects to see an isolated one or two here and there. The luggage was soon checked and in a few minutes we were running along the shore of the St Lawrence to the southwest in the direction of Lachine, and at this point we have to cross the St Lawrence in a ferryboat, a small steamer resembling some one of our third-class tugs, the passage is brief, a few minutes, but it is quite a marvel of navigation. The run is across the wake of the rapids, and the boat had to steer for a point many degrees higher up, to enable her to catch her destination the currents are so strong. But we have arrived at Caughnawaga, a small place with a large name, and evidently of Indian origin, and then a pleasant run across the prairie from the St Lawrence to Lake Champlain, some forty miles or so. Although this part is called the prairie it is of com-siderable interest on account of its fertility; Nature, in some of her most primitive aspects, is grander than when subdued by culture; on the path we have both. We have *les prairies artificielles et les prairies naturelles*, and we have an opportunity of judging of them both The forests and the savannahs along the railway, nearly across the whole way, are a profusion of strange growth to a native of this country, but the variety and richness of colour are startling and pleasing. On no part of the continent where I was could there be seen the same Indian-like luxuriance of beauty, apart from flowers themselves. The maple tree itself, on any of its sylvan accessory surroundings, forms a picture which gives richness and glowing efficacy to every succeeding landscape. The land is very level, and parts of it carefully cultivated and fully cleared. Most of the places on this line are small, some of French and some of British origin, so far as the names would indicate. By being cleared, I mean there are none or few stumps remaining in the ground, which is common in districts recently reclaimed.

I have already stated the lynx-eyed vigilance and official care which is bestowed on all who pass from Canada to the States, and I have stated at this time my course was towards the States, and now the representative of the Bald Eagle has made his appearance in the interest of Protection and Conservatism, and one can enjoy it at this stage, for it fills up a gap on a long run to very good effect, especially if you are conscious that your baggage is above any suspicion, and has no taint of "contraband" about it. However, all are regarded as guilty until they give the ocular proof that they are innocent. All who have luggage are marched down through the train to the position of the baggage car, and as the train is at full speed, the inquiry is conducted under disadvantageous circumstances, and the few who are congregated together look as if they were "half-seas over," for the car keeps shaking, and at times one passenger finds his head has come into contact with the side of the car or his neighbour's nose, and apologies are rife and reasonable too, and the officer is obliged as well as the rest to apologise, for his examination ought to have been made in the steamer while coming across the river which is the usual place for doing so, but I suppose the importance of his duty would enable him to expose the goods of the traveller at any stage on Yankee territory. The duty being done, the official at once evaporates, and we arrive at Rouse's Point, and Lake Champlain bursts upon the sight. The lake is of considerable interest, and is of great length, though it is considered small in a country where there are so many great ones. It is partly in Canada and partly in New York and Vermont States, and I think must be about two hundred miles from the upper end to its mouth at the St. Lawrence, though the narrow part of it is called the Richelieu River. The lake at some parts is fourteen miles broad, and at other parts just of sufficient breadth to allow the steamer safe navigation. From the point of starting to the head of the lake must be about one hundred and thirty miles, as it occupies about eight hours to accomplish it. After getting into the centre of the lake, a very fine and expansive view of surrounding country is got, and as we proceed upward in the lake we get into sight of a hilly country, and on that account it is sought largely by pleasure parties, for there are many fine spots which are reached by the places the steamer calls at on her passage up the lake. There are ports on both sides of the lake, and an ample opportunity is afforded to see the character of the country all the way up. Besides places and spots of interest to the tourist there is evidence of the shores of the lake being of considerable interest in a commercial point, for mines of ironstone have recently been opened, and their openings in the hillside are observable as the boat passes on her way. These openings are immediately over the navigable stream, and the barges are loaded from the mouth of the mine, and on the nearest point of land to the mine, where suitable ground is obtained for furnaces for manufacturing the iron. There are works in course of erection, and some have been in operation for some

time. These ironworks are principally on one side of
the lake. There is one place of considerable importance called Burlington, and though one cannot see
the whole extent of the place by passing, yet there is
as much visible from the pier as will give a very
prominent notion of lively industry from the amount
of vapour which rises and is emitted from the various
works in sight. Great piles of timber are observable
on the foreshore, and I daresay the works are chiefly
engaged in cutting and preparing timber for the
market. There are railways nearly all round the
shore, with the exception of a portion of the hilliest
and rockiest shore, and they are now supplying that
want. For in passing up I noticed very many steam
drills at work boring the rock before blasting. The
rocks all along are either granite or white, and at some
points it looks rather serious work, on account of the
bold, irregular outline of the rock. The lake is not
suited for heavy shipping, the vessels which are seen
are all of the character of coasting crafts. There are
several localities in the interior which are reached by
the lake shore and are great resorts for pleasure
seekers. The first of these is the village of Plattsburg, which is the name for the wilderness, but I am
not sure that there are many similarities also take
advantage of these solitudes. The next is more
likely to get a greater amount of patrons for by the
station of Port Kent tourists reach the fishing lakes.

which are near to the Adirondack Mountains, a locality of great interest to the tourist, both on account of its rural beauty and its piscatorial pleasures. There is another station, which has an Indian name, and from these the tourist proceeds by coach to visit the fairy lake and scenery on Lake George. This small and beautiful lake is a tributary of the large lake, but there is no passage by its stream, and when the steamer arrives at Ticonderoga, they must either proceed on foot or by the stage for some three miles across a rather interesting country. The general look of the country from this part of the lake is calculated to please the most critical. Surrounding, there seems a circle of picturesque and wooded hills, whose tops present a succession of nicely-rounded lines, but none of them seen from the lake are of any height, but well-clothed with trees, which look finely from the lake; but one misses on some of the ample plateau the lovely mansion embowered in the bosom of tall ancestral trees, with winding avenues and walks and soft borders of *tapis vert*. After we have proceeded a hundred miles or so up the lake it narrows to little more than the breadth of the steamer, and the land in the vicinity assumes the appearance of some of our own Highland lochs. The hills get a little more peaked, and rise more steeply from the water side; some parts are thickly wooded, and on the most barren spots

there is evidence of considerable fertility. We have
passed every kind of craft on the way up which
frequent this lake. Steamers start from both ends
at morning and night, and there is a continuous
course of navigation going on. Rafts of considerable
size are seen wending their way to St. Lawrence on
their way to Quebec. Lines of flat, scow-looking
boats are loaded with lighter kinds of lumber, light
vessels loaded with grain, and lighter boats engaged
in various pursuits by the banks of the lake; but
when the steamer appears there is a profound panic
observable, for its great size affects the water to
such an extent in the narrow parts of the lake
that the boatmen have to use great exertions to
save their boats from destruction. We have passed
along this narrow part of the lake, possibly twenty
or thirty miles, where much nautical skill is necessary to keep clear of the land at the sides and the
mud at the bottom. We have turned many corners
and promontories with many curious kinds of pharos
by the way; and we got into the dull and sluggish
water at the very top of the lake, and we sight
Whitehall, our destination, as it nestles between two
Alpine walls of imposing height, and in the valley runs
the canal which was the old connecting highway between the St Lawrence and the Hudson River, unit-
ing New York with its own capital Albany and the
Canadian cities on the east by Lake Champlain

CHAPTER XIX.

WHITEHALL, SARATOGA, AND ALBANY.

IT would require some time to discover another place of similar character, so far as topographical features are concerned, like Whitehall. The valley on which it is set is of great extent, and in this respect totally unlike great numbers of American places, it being at the junction of the lake and the canal, and also in the centre of a thickly-wooded country. One of the outlets will show a sufficient reason why such a place exists there, for at that part the country is strikingly alpine and confined, and the houses in some instances rise one above another, but the place generally has a snug and comfortable look. The train near to this place passes through a tunnel, which is rather an uncommon occurrence, and the only one which I remember on that side of the continent, but the hills are evidently huddled together on this part, for we soon loose the hilly country and keep driving along the banks of the canal for a considerable time, and when the country opens up one discovers that it has been subjected to culture for a long time, for now and then large and comfortable farms are passed, looking like some of our better class houses and surroundings at

home. Fields and forests and all along the sides of
the canals are proofs of much labour being carried on
in connection with agriculture. Numerous villages
are passed and now and again a place of some importance, and the nearer to the great centre we approach
the more enterprising and interesting does the country
become. The iron which is found in the district of
Champlain finds its way up into the land in this
locality, and there are various places where extensive
works are carried on, one of these called Mechanics-
ville is quite suggestive though nothing more be said.

The great centre of attraction in this portion of the
country is the fashionable resort called Saratoga, with
its hotels, springs, promenades, charming villas, and
its fashionable station and aristocratic aroma of the
beau monde. There is no difficulty of discovering,
when one approaches, the environs of this place for
there is nothing in the States which can be converted
into cents but affords a speculative medium for
Yankee enterprise. The water of the various springs
around this resort are utilised, and brought into the
trains for sale, so that those who are too much pressed
for time to go to the waters have the waters brought
to them; but I saw no one who was disposed to go
in for the Saratoga *eau-de-vie*. In almost all American
places of any extent the hotel life is a feature, and the
hotels a prominent one especially in this place, and
although there are many here of great capacity, these

T

have been found to be insufficient for the great increase or demand made upon them at this growing place. At present they are engaged constructing one which will hold nearly all the contents of the others put together, and will of itself be an attraction inducing greater traffic. This is regarded by all as the most celebrated watering-place in the United States. As with the middle or store-keeping class, *la nation boutiquiere*, horse and buggy is the acme of possession and enjoyment, so with the upper ten to go to Saratoga or Longbranch is the very summit of social felicity. All eyes and hearts, from the autocrat whose days and nights are spent in the national caravansary at Washington, to the wealthy oyster merchant whose chief cares are centred on some of the beds of that shellfish in New York Bay during *la mauvaise saison* in which his money is made, but whose recess is in the time of year when life is joyous at such places as those I have named; and the lake is just a fine drive out some seven miles. Boating and fishing at the lake is an enhanced enjoyment, and hotel facilities are afforded for those who wish to prolong their stay at such enjoyable quarters. The scenery is so different from what is to be seen at Longbranch that it offers a most decided change. At the one you gaze on the wide expanse of the ocean, with its hoarse music and fitful breeze, or its calm and dazzling light quivering with the surges from the Atlantic's strife, and busy

with the craft and flags of every nation passing in
steady procession to the busy harbour of New York.
At the other you have the same radiant shoals of
fashionable life, crowding round the parks, the springs,
the palatial mansions, the verdant slopes, the refresh-
ing fountains, admiring the aerial creations deep in
the crystal lake, or sitting upon the banks and uplands
and regaling themselves with the odour from the
flowers, or listening to the natural music from the
groves around, or to the song of the young amateurs
as they draw their gondolas through the rippling
waves of their tiny ocean.

But we pass this fashionable paradise and come to
a place of classic name. Troy is one of those bustling
maelstroms of industry which are to be met or passed
rather, on our way to the capital of the State of New
York. There are many places along the line which
are evidently the seats of lively industry, but as the
practice of naming stations is not generally pursued
in the States, strangers must be at a loss to learn
them, if they do not wish to be considered inquisitive; but it is very necessary to be so. When one is
in quest of knowledge or information, all the obstacles
which present themselves must be pushed to one
side, so long as that can be done without knocking
anybody down. However, in doing so some inter-
rogation is apt to be perceived as compensation for the
favour some one has done you in answering a query,

or a succession of queries, "What do you think of our country?" is sure to be the first, whatever may succeed. "We have no poor people in our country;" this is very often the second. Of course such a statement as that is very noble, if true, if they prevent people from becoming poor; for my own part, I was inclined to look upon the statement, "The poor ye have always with you," as one of universal application and thoroughly true. But it seems there are parts in the States where there are no poor people. I thought he might be speaking of the place where his lot was cast. I must admit I saw no poor people where I was, but I have no doubt there are plenty of them in New York, or any of the large cities. In recent settlements there was every likelihood of few being there. But I think it is usually intended for a thrust relative to the state of things in our own country at home. However, my reply was that "I thought when his country was as old as the mother country they were likely to have plenty of poor people among them." But I have no desire, nevertheless, that they should have such a prophetic statement verified. It will be best for all, and I don't care much for my reputation as a prophet. May it be long ere "hungry ruin has them in the wind." In districts of country where there is a large agricultural population, the people are in a favourable position to live well; for in any part of the States food

in the agricultural portions is less costly than in the
cities, and nearly a half of the prices charged in cities
at home.

I have referred to the system and advantage of
checking the luggage of travellers and tourists generally on the American continent. Whether one's
baggage is much or little, great or small, it should be
checked in passing from place to place when it is not
wanted. It costs nothing, and when wanted at any
stage it is as sure to be where it is wanted as if it
was in the care of a person whose duty was to look
after it alone. In commencing the journey I had
omitted to get my baggage checked as it was
handy, and I thought I could look after it, which
can always be done provided there is plenty of time
to do so; but in the case of shifting for a different
rail or steamer sometimes there is much hurry and
bustle, and if at night, as sometimes will happen,
there is a hurry to get the baggage sent forward for
a change, and that having the official care will necessarily receive the first attention, but there is a
remedy for this. Some time before we arrived at
Albany, a person, not official I concluded, came and
made inquiry whether all the luggage was checked,
and having stated mine was not so, he desired to
take it in charge, and when I consented, he gave me
a card or check, and made a charge which I thought
exorbitant for the duty to be rendered, but by the

advice of one of my co-travellers I was induced to accept the services which I by a little forethought might have rendered unnecessary; but it is well that there is some agency to assist and direct strangers, though primarily the motive which prompts is purely of a commercial character. On arriving at the station at Albany, which is a place of considerable importance, there was very much bustle on the part of those who were prosecuting their travel to a greater distance, and who were necessitated to change. Very many like myself were about to proceed down the north river or the Hudson to New York, by the steamer St. John, which was waiting at her berth, and as the train was late the excitement was some degrees more intense than had she arrived in time; but shortly all the 'busses, cabs, or cars got filled, and we drove off along what seemed to me to be a succession of badly made streets, to the pier, where an excess of stir, of light and animated crowds, indicated that we had arrived at our destination.

CHAPTER XX

THE HUDSON AND ITS FLOATING PALACES AND SCENERY.

THE despatch of the steamers which ply on the Hudson seems to be an event of some interest to the folk at Albany, if one were to judge from the numbers which crowd to see them off; but as the passengers are numerous, so are the friends likely to be who accompany them to the pier. The passenger is either the steerer on the corpo deck, which is below the saloon on the forepart of the boat, and the saloon is reached by a flight of steps from the lower deck to the saloon. The ticket-office is on the lower deck, and the quarters for the night are secured by applying to the clerk, and when that is done you ascend to the saloon above, and from this point the quality of the upper portion of the vessel is discovered. At the bottom of the stairs stand two figures, one on each side, just at the scroll of the hand rail. These figures are made of bronze, and they are set on pedestals of the same material and in the hands of the figures are gas burners, lighting the way up stairs. The stair itself is composed of Californian red wood, or a hard wood of corresponding colour. Each step is set into a landing framework of considerable strength, and the brackets between the steps are of a suitably ornamental construction, and all highly polished, and the appearance of the whole is pleasing, light, and highly ornamental. On the landing, before entering the saloon, the name of the steamer is indented with polished brass. On entering the saloon one feels as if he had got into wrong quarters, the general appearance to a British eye is so unlike a ship. The saloon is about 300 feet in length, and the whole can be taken in at a glance from stem to stern, and it presented the appearance of a ball-room, at least it did so to some extent when I first entered. When the usual bustle of starting is going on, and passengers are busy getting their luggage put away into their state-rooms, and various other incidental and necessary acts were being gone about, there is much animation and lively commotion; and the scene is of much interest and calculated to attract attention on account of its extent and magnificence. The saloon being of great length necessitates it being of great height, and from its construction materially adds to the interior magnificence of the place. The ceiling is over twenty-two feet high, and its form, as seen from the inside, is eliptical, and is supported in the centre by five pillars, which are about equi-distant. These pillars are Corinthian in style, with fluted shafts, and the capitals are about three feet in size and richly gilded. Running down through the

centre of the saloon and between the pillars are five
immense gaseliers, about eight or ten feet across at
the lustres. These hang from the centre of the
ceiling to about nine or ten feet from the deck, and
to preserve them from damage on account of the
steamer's motion, there are ornamental chains or
cords, which are fastened to the side galleries. On
each of these gaseliers are from fifteen to twenty
globes, and so many lights make the saloon extremely
light, cheerful, and enjoyable. The ceiling, as I have
indicated, curves gently towards the sides, and at the
ends of the moulding or beam dividing the panels on
the ceiling, and between these beams, which are
some two feet apart, are stained-glass skylights of a
variety of designs and colour, which give a very
sparkling and shining radiance to the light in the
daytime. Round the entire sides of the hall, arcade,
or saloon, for it looks like all of these, are between
200 and 300 berths for the accommodation and comfort of the travellers. These are disposed in two
tiers one above the other, and between, say ten feet
high, are galleries or balconies, which run round the
whole extent of the ship, terminating at each end
like an upper deck or entersole; and from these one
can pass out to the open deck from both ends of the
steamer. On the inner side of the galleries is a railing or balustrade, very nicely executed, and adding
very much to the interest of the internal arrange-

ments of the steamer. In the centre or near to the centre of the saloon there is a double descent from the side galleries to a broad stair which connects with the main deck of the saloon, and on several prominent angles of the stairway there are some fine bronze figures of considerable artistic merit, which tend to enhance the most unique and stately surroundings that are to be seen at every turn. Near to this part of the boat there is the only structure which prevents the saloon from being one clear space from stem to stern. That is the woodwork enclosing the lower part of the beam which rises from the lower or cargo deck to the upper or hurricane deck or roof, but to obviate any objectionable tendency arising from the existence of the enclosure, the sides of it are filled up in the same manner in mock woodwork as if it were entrances to state-rooms, and on parts of it are mirrors which give it a light and agreeable look. At the bases of all the pillars are circles of settees, and sofas, lounges, and chairs are set up in all available places, and all the floors are covered with carpets of heavy fabric. The doors at entrances of all the berths or state-rooms are specimens of tasteful workmanship, with moulding and carving of superior make, and showily painted and gilded, and over them are ventilators of cut fretwork, of elaborately curious openings, imparting an airy character to that part of the steamer.

After what I have said of the interior of the steamer, one can easily conceive what has been said of these vessels to be true: that many travel on them purely for pleasure, and the various pleasures obtainable and purchasable on board, and the extreme probable of certain seasons [illegible] of [illegible] [illegible] to attract the [illegible], the [illegible], and the travelers who love the charms of gay life on the Hudson, or love to roam among the fascinating sceneries of Manhattan's Island, which is the [illegible] [illegible] that absorbs the vigour, the vitality, and the virtue of the [illegible] surrounding places. When I went on board the St. Johns the whole saloon was basking in a blaze of brilliant gas light, and all the [illegible] on every side was filled with a throng of every shade of character. [illegible] the tables were little knots of ladies reading, chatting, sewing and knitting; others promenading the galleries, and [illegible] and [illegible] their centre of action for the evening also; others were regaling themselves with the fresh breeze from the Hudson which played round the verandah on the upper deck. On the lower deck all were congregated a [illegible] company of [illegible] spirits, engaged in [illegible] a [illegible] [illegible] to their [illegible] forth his [illegible] [illegible] retorts, and the unvarying hand [illegible] and this continued till [illegible] [illegible] that hour of [illegible]'s [illegible] [illegible] the key alone had arrived. By that time [illegible] had retired within the confines of [illegible] [illegible]," or a

the steamer pursued her course so steadily and smoothly that it was difficult to discover in some parts of the ship that she moved at all, so steady is the stroke from the engines of these steamers. We have seen what like these vessels are on the upper or saloon deck, now let us take a step to the lower or cargo deck. From the bottom of the stair leading to the saloon forward is devoted to cargo chiefly, but over and above we have the boiler, and in the centre the engines, and a gaswork at one side also. The boilers are placed, one on starboard and the other on the larboard sides of the steamer, just in the vicinity of the paddles, and this arrangement internally gives the vessel externally that look which is peculiarly American, that of having a funnel at each side. All the deck except a needful passage is loaded with cargo usually, and a number of what we would call steerage passengers are quartered about, as this is the only place where they can stow themselves away, and being in the vicinity of the fires, it is comfortable in the winter, I presume; but in the fine season they can look out upon the river from the gangway as the vessel passes on her voyage. There in a deck below this again, where all refreshments are dispensed, and where all the cooking goes on, the officials and attendants being darkies chiefly, quiet, civil, and attentive in their deportment and labours. These dining saloons are very cheerful in the even-

ing, and being lighted up with gas are quite lively
and enjoyable. The capacity of these steamers for
passengers' comfort is very great; every place has
the same character for amplitude and convenience.
The deck space outside is rather limited, there is but
a small space comparatively at the stem and the
same at the stern, where the passengers can enjoy the
view in sailing down the river, and these are very
much crowded on that account. There is no possi-
bility of seeing out from the saloon of the steamer,
as state-rooms and berths are ranged two deep the
whole length of the ship, and there is no allowance
given to go up on the upper deck or roof of the
saloon, so to speak, which is a considerable height
above the water line, and would be somewhat uncom-
fortable on that account. There are no masts or
sails about these ships, and it is almost unnecessary
to call them either ships, boats, or vessels as the
same we understand it. There are upright poles
at certain parts of the steamer, and there are guys
or stays that run along from them to certain of
the strongest portions of the vessel to steady or
strengthen her, and whether these are the cause of
relieving the steamer from the ordinary vibration
which is common in steamships or not I cannot say,
but there is no such thing felt in the ship while on
the passage and this along with the other facts
which I have stated, is the reason why these vessels

are so highly spoken of by many persons of position and judgment as a source of much pleasure to travellers who use them on this and the other favourite routes in America.

Whilst there is thus every attention paid to the comfort of those who patronize these vessels for the purpose of pleasure or business, there is also due regard to and provision made for their safety in the event of fire or wrecks. In various parts of the steamer are life-belts or preservers in sufficient number for the passengers, and there are instructions exposed about the vessel how these are to be used, and the process is as simple as the appliance seems to be. They are made of cork, in the form of small blocks tied together in a line, and are thrown over the shoulder and fastened in much the same manner as one would do a vest or jacket, and I suppose these keep up the unfortunates who are obliged to test them practically till aid reaches them from the shore or steamers. Then, for the calamity of fire, the directions chiefly apply to the crew, detailing the manner in which they are to act, and the manner of those with whom they are to act in concert. I presume these arrangements will entail a drill of some sort which they will all have previously acquired, and which is doubtless very necessary and proper. The first feeling which disturbs one on these night voyages is the apprehension of fire. The knowledge

that there is a work for the manufacture of gas on
board, a gasometer and pipes permeating the entire
vessel with their inflammable contents, and every
place lighted brilliantly, only bespeak the startling
transformation if anything were going wrong.

I visited almost every corner of the ship and
watched all the changing aspects of life presented in
this short voyage. The brilliant and dazzling appearance of the saloon faded away gradually as the
ebony-coloured official extinguished one by one the
flaming ministers which encircled the ponderous
gasaliers, and, lastly, the immensity of the long and
yawning emptiness of the saloon became painfully
silent and deserted, and looked the very picture of
solitude, which was only broken occasionally by the
steamer's shrill whistle as it sounded its warning note
to some approaching ship, which echoed in return its
responsive blast, and anon its sound was hushed as it
floated over the waters of the lordly Hudson.

I have delayed making any reference to steamers
up to this point, as I thought the Hudson or North
River the most suitable relation in which to speak of
them, because it was on this river in 1807 that Robert
Fulton first gave the world the solar proof that
steam could be applied in such a way as to be one
of the first scientific appearances for the good of
mankind, and we who live only seven years after
that date know how fully the hopes and aspirations

of that great engineer have been realised. It is a little singular, however, that in the country where the first advances were made in the practical application of this important art they should have been so unsuccessful in its promotion, compared with what has been realised by those who were their followers. It is not my intention at present to state any reasons why the Clyde has taken the first place in connection with all the enterprise which has been evinced in promoting the industries which have secured such a prominence, and which have caused all the world to think and speak highly of the marine architecture produced on our river, and we are not to suppose that that is the result of a beneficent and benign prerogative which we enjoy, of being surrounded by a halo from the manes of the great Watt. There may be something in a name, but the rebellious and turbulent waters of the Atlantic pay no attention to the ideal qualifications which are secured by anything so unsubstantial and unreal; and when the productions of the Delaware can cope with those of the Clyde, there will be a change of prestige, despite our present eminence. Of course we might console ourselves with the knowledge of the fact that we had instructed their fingers to fight against us in the friendly battle of competition; but this is a little away from my text. The noble river on which we are embarked is striking, on account of its scenery as well as its steamers or floating palaces, and it is interesting on account of its historic associations. We have passed a large part of it in the dark, but it is the part which is allowed to be most lacking in that which I have indicated. The whole extent of this trip is about one hundred and sixty miles from Albany to New York. In coming down we pass the district where the great city is supplied with water, which is forty miles from New York. The place is called Croton, and the aqueduct and reservoir are objects of considerable interest. These waterworks cost nearly three millions sterling. The dam or lake is about five miles long, it covers four hundred acres, and the discharge from the lake is about sixty million gallons daily. The water is carried through a canal for forty miles, and the canal is built of stone and brick; and the receiving reservoir which is about five miles from the centre of New York, is capable of containing one hundred and fifty million gallons. This reservoir is wholly an artificial work, and is built in the Egyptian style of architecture, with massive buttresses all round, and on the top of the wall is an enclosed promenade. By these works the great city is amply supplied with water —the drainage of the country in the vicinity of Croton exceeding a hundred miles, with numerous small lakes. I don't wish the reader to suppose this is all part of the scenery of the Hudson, but I have been led to refer to the whole work on account of passing

v

the site of the reservoirs; and I may as well refer to another structure connected with these works which is over the stream where the Island of Manahattan terminates, just at the burying-place of Anthony Van Corlear, at *Spuyten Duryel Creek*. At this place is what is called the High Bridge which carries the Croton water across the Harlem River. This bridge spans the valley where the river is six hundred feet wide and the valley a quarter of a mile or so. It has eight arches of eighty feet span, and they are a hundred feet high above the water line, but the arches on the land diminish with the slopes of the land. This bridge is wholly composed of granite, and the water is led over it in iron pipes extending for fourteen hundred and fifty feet, and there is a pathway, which is broad enough for a carriage, but only foot passengers are allowed to pass. We had passed "Sleepy Hollow," when the gray curtain of morning was rising drowsily from its quiet and silent slopes, but did not see any of the "Winkles" on the lookout. On all the way down from the point which the celebrated navigator for whom the river was called, reached on his first voyage up, or the point at which the chain or barrier was thrown across during the Revolution, is of marked interest and attraction in natural beauties, bristling in legendary lore, and teeming with the most cherished historic association of the early days of the Republic and of the struggles

and endurance of the martyrs of liberty, of which it
is impossible to do more than to refer to in a passing
and transitory manner. At one point we pass the
district from which the granite palaces of the city are
constructed, with its bold and irregular masses jutting
overhead, and again we are charmed by the verdant
woody slopes of "Sunnyside," the residence of
Washington Irving; then a fort is passed, and
then a village and scores of sylvan retreats, the
residences of the merchants of New York. We catch
a hurried glimpse of some magnificent buildings
devoted to beneficent or charitable purposes, and as
we approach, the grand imposing features of the
river, the majestic and towering palisades, in some
parts so like those basaltic and irregular gigantic
masses of rock at Giant's Causeway, we are at
once rivetted with their surpassing magnificence.
When we were passing, the warm, golden radiance of
the morning sun was beginning to stimulate the
dewy vapour into motion, and as the snowy curtain
began to rise and ascend to the towering battlements
of these everlasting walls, and roll along their sum-
mits in volutes of downy white, the picture was one
among a thousand. On the slope below and near to
the margin of the lovely Hudson were numbers of
beautiful mansions embowered in vernal beauty and
halcyon repose, while in the background rose the
wild and romantic rocky escarpment, surrounding

and encircling little frescoes here and there on the shelves of the dizzy heights. At anchor in their little glassy bays numerous yachts were waiting for their gay holiday trappings and pleasure-seeking crowds. The rocky heights recede, and their beauty and rugged grandeur are softened and mellowed into romantic indistinctness. The Elysian fields of Hoboken run into their retreats of quiet and modest natural profusion, and the varied beauties of nature are fresh and sparkling with new life. The islands of New York Bay are now in view; villas and villages are thickening, the highlands are robed in the cool shadows, the river and the bay are glowing with a mixture of purple and golden light, and long, deep sombre shadows tremble between the water and the land, and lose themselves in the radiance of the lake.

The early trains begin to roll along the eastern bank, and startle with their shrill pipe the echoes on its rocky sides. The screaming and fitful vapours from dozens of public works denote that we are near our journey's end. The busy wharves and ferries are reached, and the bay of New York, with its islands, forts, and public works, and fair foreshore, its restless commerce, and sleepless activity and princely possessions, is at last before us, and around us New York on the left and New Jersey on the right. The wharf at which the Hudson River steamers lie is almost the most northerly, that is, the one farthest up on the

west side of New York, and is nearly three miles up
the North River, reckoning from Battery Point which
is the extreme south point of the island of Manhattan,
and on the opposite shore of Jersey. There are great
numbers of docks, wharves, ferries and basins, reaching
for about as many miles, and on the east side of
New York, at the entrance to the East River, and on
the Brooklyn shore, there are as many more, and this
extent of foreshore seen at once from the bay with all
its relative bustle and enterprise causes it to be one
of the liveliest scenes of maritime life and activity
which can be seen anywhere, and in the bay there is
always seen a stream of inward-bound and outward-
bound vessels of all kinds and dimensions, and to and
from every nation and clime on earth, and as the
aspect in the bay is so varied, so is life in the city
itself, and is naturally similar to what is observable
in any of our large ports in Britain. But I think the
excessive bustle which one sees about the wharves,
and in the vicinity of the shipping, is the result of
such work being done in so limited a space, for the
shores of New York, on which these labours of business are carried on are just two sides of a triangle,
the Battery being the point, and as it is found to be
more convenient to form wharves and docks on the
opposite sides of New Jersey and Brooklyn than to
extend them up the North and East Rivers, this also
has a tendency to concentrate the business done in

New York to that old part of the city, and the social as well as the commercial tendencies are the same in relation to the centre of business. Brooklyn will extend with greater rapidity now than will New York itself, although the facilities for getting at the one are as manifold as the other. The Central Park, which I have already referred to, lies at the present northern confines of the city, and it is evidently in contemplation of the completion of the city it was so named, for at present it has no such relation to the city itself, and thus its name has an enormously prospective relation to the future only.

There were some things which I referred to in rather a summary manner when noticing the appearance of New York Bay at landing, and among these I referred to the gigantic undertaking of spanning the East River with an immense granite bridge, the piers of which are nearly 200 feet high, and the span is of such dimensions that it will not interfere with the navigation of the river; but above this bridge, on the same river, there is another mighty enterprise in operation, that of removing a mass of sunken rock which renders the navigation at that point rather dangerous. This enterprise has been going on for years, and will proceed for over two years to come. It is tunnelled from the land, and an immense cavern or crypt is formed by cutting and blasting the rock in the interior, and when the engineers think there a sufficient material removed, a great quantity of gunpowder will be placed inside, and the upper crust will be blown to atoms and the channel of the river be improved. This great event will take place on the centennial celebration of the nation's independence in 1876, and I suppose is intended a part of the programme which will be gone into. I don't know that these will be calculated in Britain, and in case they should not be so I have been thus particular to call attention to it before I leave these shores, so that those who wish to be present at such an imposing and startling exhibition will know when to cross the Atlantic to visit the shores of the New World.

THE END

www.ingramcontent.com/pod-product-compliance
Lightning Source LLC
Chambersburg PA
CBHW022027240426
43667CB00042B/1213